Jacob:
Wrestling with God

By
Rev. F. B. Meyer

AMG Publishers™

Chattanooga, TN 37422

Jacob:
Wrestling with God

Originally published by
the Fleming H. Revell Company in New York.

ISBN 0-89957-182-4

Printed in the United States of America
06 05 04 03 02 01–R–6 5 4 3 2 1

Contents

Foreword

F. B. Meyer's *Jacob: Wrestling with God* is an inspiring biography of one of the greatest Old Testament patriarchs. In delineating the life of Jacob, Meyer presents insightful homilies regarding the events of Jacob's life and the roles he played in God's divine plan for His people.

We at AMG Publishers have made a few minor changes to the original work to help make its content more clear to modern readers: We have updated spelling and some archaic terms in accordance with how our language has changed over the years; in some cases, unusual forms of punctuation have been simplified in order to eliminate confusion. Readers should note that the points of current history mentioned by Meyer are from the latter half of nineteenth-century England.

It is our hope that readers will be moved by the wisdom in these chapters to seek a deeper knowledge and understanding of God's Word.

Preface

It was the custom with some of the older commentators to write as though their loyalty to God's Spirit required that they should show that the acts of the Old Testament saints were all of them consistent with the highest morality. This was especially evident in their remarks on the career of the patriarch whose name stands on our title page. Ingenious attempts have been made to palliate episodes and transactions in his life, which at first sight certainly conflict with our conceptions of righteousness.

It was this that led me in the first instance to prepare this book. I wrote it with the avowed purpose of telling the story of Jacob's life, extenuating nothing; portraying his failures as well as his victories; and endeavoring to show that the Word of God does not hesitate to describe the imperfections and native deformities of its most conspicuous characters, because of the incalculable benefit which may accrue in the two following directions.

First, mankind is taught that the love of God is not determined by what it finds in man. God loves, not because we are good, but to make us so. He is not surprised by the evil He discovers in us, and His lovingkindness is not turned away by our sin.

Secondly, it is a great comfort to find that the saints of Bible story were men of like passions with ourselves; and if God was able to shape materials so rough into vessels so fair, there is hope that He will not fail nor be discouraged until He has done the like for us.

It will also be a great pleasure if these pages will serve to show some of my fellow workers, weary with the incessant demands of their congregations, how they may find a constant wellspring of freshness, variety, and interest, in the glorious biographies of Scripture. To recruit a dwindling congregation; to sustain interest in a crowded one; to awaken new devotion to the Bible; and to touch the many chords of human life—there is nothing to be compared with a reverent retelling of the stories of Bible Heroes and Saints.

F. B. meyer.

☙ 1

First Impressions

Genesis 25

One adequate support
For the calamities of mortal life
Exists—one only: an assured belief
That the procession of our fate, however
Sad or disturbed, is ordered by a Being
Of Infinite benevolence and power;
Whose everlasting purposes embrace
All accidents, converting them to good
Wordsworth

A n old-world story this! In its strange Eastern dress, it appears to be as remote from us as the garb of an Arab, or the barter of an Oriental bazaar. And yet human life is much the same, whether lived eighteen hundred years on this side or eighteen hundred years on that side of the Cross; whether hidden beneath our broadcloth, or the flowing robes of an Arab Sheikh; whether spent in modern towns, or on the free, open pasture lands of Southern Palestine.

Our critics complain of our poring over these time-worn pages of ancient biography, but, with all deference to them, we feel bound to say that we learn better how to live, we inhale more spiritual ozone, we see further into the reasons of God's dealings with men, when doing so, than when scanning the pages of yesterday's newspaper, or of a society journal.

With human life and discipline, one day is as a thousand years, and a thousand years as one day. Souls grasp hands across the intervening centuries. Thousands of miles cannot part us from our kin across the seas; and thousands of years cannot part us from our kin across the ages, or sever the readers of these words—who daily weep over an often dropped ideal—from that son of Isaac, who, nearly drowned in the seas of his own craft and cunning, at length emerged a new man, and a prince with God.

There are many reasons which invest this story with absorbing interest:

I. JACOB WAS THE FATHER OF THE JEWISH RACE, AND A TYPICAL JEW. The Jews called themselves by the name of Jacob; and surnamed themselves by the name of Israel (Is. 44:5). God calls them children of Israel. We call them Israelites. We speak of Jacob, rather than Abraham, as the founder of the people to which he gave his name, because, though Abraham was their ancestor, yet he was no so exclusively. He is the founder of a yet richer, mightier line. The wild son of the desert claims him as father equally with the bargain-loving Jew. Nor is that all. We Gentiles have reason to be proud to trace back our lineage to the first great Hebrew, the man who *crossed over*,* and whom God designated as His friend. He is the father of all who believe: not of the circumcision only, but of those who walk in the steps of the faith which he had, even before he was circumcised (Rom. 4:12). *We* go to make up the sands on the shore and the stars of the heavens, which he saw in the vision of God (Gen. 22:17).

But Jacob is the typical Jew. His life is the epitome of that wonderful people, who are found in every country and belong to none; who supply us with our loftiest religious literature, and are yet a byword for their craft, their scheming, and their love of money; who have supplied us with our highest ideals of nobility, and our lowest types of villainy; who have played so great a part in the history of the past, and are only waiting now for the final catastrophe which is to replace them in the van of the world's progress.

No thoughtful man can ignore this wonderful people. Their history is, without doubt, the key to the complications of modern politics; and it may be that their redemption is to be the fruit of that mighty tra-

---

*The word "Hebrew," according to the generally-accepted interpretation, signifies *the man who had crossed the river-flood*—the man who came from beyond the Euphrates. (See Stanley's *Jewish Church*, i, p. 10.)

vail, which is beginning to convulse all peoples, announced as it is, by throes of earthquake and the rumors of war.

If we can understand the life of Jacob, we can understand the history of his people. The extremes which startle us in them are all in him. Like them, he is the most successful schemer of his times; and, like them, he has that deep spirituality and that far-seeing faith which are the grandest of all qualities, and make a man capable of the highest culture that a human spirit can receive. Like them, he spends the greatest part of his life in exile, and amid trying conditions of toil and sorrow; and, like them, he is inalienably attached to that dear land, his only hold on which was by the promise of God and the graves of the heroic dead.

But Jacob's character was purified by tremendous discipline. The furnace into which he was cast was heated one seven times more than it is wont to be heated for ordinary men. He stands among the peers in the kingdom of sorrow; and through it all he passed into a peerage of moral and spiritual power, which made the mightiest monarch of his times bend eagerly for a blessing from his trembling hand. Through such discipline his people have been passing for centuries; and surely, before its searching fires, the baser elements of their natures will be expelled, until they recognize the true Joseph of their seed—who has sent them many generous gifts; whom yet they have not known, but towards whom they are certainly being brought. Then shall they share His glory (Gen. 45:13, 18); and they shall be among many people, "as a dew from the Lord" (Mic. 5:7); yea, in them shall be fulfilled the ancient promise, "I will bless thee; and thou shalt be a blessing" (Gen. 12:2).

II. JACOB ALSO HAS SO MANY POINTS OF CONTACT WITH OURSELVES. Newman has said truly, "Abraham was a hero; Jacob was a plain man dwelling in tents. Abraham we feel to be above ourselves; Jacob like ourselves. We no longer stand in the unclouded golden dawn of the patriarchal age; it is overcast with clouds, and is more like our own checkered life."

His *failings* speak to us. He takes advantage of his brother when hard pressed with hunger. He deceives his father. He meets Laban's guile with guile. He thinks to buy himself out of his trouble with Esau. He mixes, in a terrible mingle-mangle, religion and worldly policy. His children grow up to hatred, violence, and murder. He cringes before the distant Egyptian governor, and sends him a present. Mean, crafty and weak, are the least terms we can apply to him. But, alas! who is there that does not feel the germs of this harvest to be within his own breast, hidden there as seed germs in a mummy case, and only waiting for favorable conditions to ripen them to the same disastrous groth. "There goes myself, but for the grace of God."

His *aspirations* speak to us. We, too, have our angel-haunted dreams, and make our vows when we leave home. We, too, count hard work a trifle, when inspired by all-mastering love. We, too, cling in a paroxysm of yearning to the departing angels, that they should bless us ere they go. We, too, get back to our Bethels, and bury our idols. We, too, confess ourselves pilgrims and strangers on the earth. We, too, recognize the shepherd care of God (Gen. 48:15). We, too, wait for God's salvation (Gen. 49:18).

His *sorrows* speak to us. In every life there is a leaving home to go forth alone; and a weary struggle for existence; and a limp which reminds us of some awful crisis; and an Allon-bachuth (an oak of weeping, Gen. 35:8); and a lonely grave on the way to Ephrath, which holds some priceless jewel case; and a lost Joseph; and the grey hairs of sorrow. And we have mourned over hopes, which have mocked us with their non-fulfillment; "I have not attained" (Gen. 47:9).

What a comfort it is to find that the Bible saints, who now shine as stars in the firmament of heaven, were men of like passions with ourselves! They were not always saints; they sinned, and murmured, and rebelled—as we do. Heaven's rarest blades were not wrought of finer metal than that which is within our constitution. God's choicest vessels were not turned from superior earth to that of which we are made. The jewels which now lie at the foundation of the new Jerusalem were once obscure, unnamed men of no finer texture than ourselves. Look to the quarry whence they were hewn, and the hold of the pit whence they were digged; and say if there was much to choose between their origin and your own. And then, take heart; for if God were able to take up such men as Jacob, and Simon Bar-Jona, and make of them princes and kings, surely He can do as much for you. The discipline may be keen as fire, but the result shall be glorious: and all eternity shall ring with the praises of Him who raises up the poor out of the dust, and lifts up the beggar from the dunghill, and makes them kings and priests unto God.

III. IN JACOB WE CAN TRACE THE WORKINGS OF DIVINE LOVE. "Jacob have I loved" (Mal. 1:2). It was *pre-natal* love. Before the child was born, it was the object of God's love (Rom. 9:11). In God's heart all his members were written, when as yet there was none of them. Though God forecasted his disposition and habits, yet He loved him. It is ever sweet to rest on a love which is dated not in time but eternity, because one feels that as God's love did not originate in any unforeseen flash of excellence in us, so it will not be turned away by any unexpected outbreak of depravity. It did not begin because of what we were; and it will continue in spite of what we are.

It was *fervent* love. So strong that, in comparison, the love which shone around Esau might be almost termed hatred (Rom. 9:13). For God loved Esau as he loves all men. He hates nothing that He has made. But there were as many degrees of temperature between His love to Jacob and that to Esau, as there are in human hearts between love and hate. Sometimes in an early morning the moon shines in the same sky as the sun—her beams still fall on all things, but one might almost assert that she did not shine, by reason of the brilliance of his beams. So was it with these two men. And who shall find faith? There must be degrees in the love of God. Was there not one disciple "whom Jesus loved?" (See also Matt. 10:37 and Luke 14:26).

It was a *disciplinary* love. We have low thoughts of love. *We* can only count that as love which caresses, and soothes, and says sweet things, and makes of itself a shield so that no rough wind may breathe on us. We have no notion of a love that can say, "No"; that can use the rod, and scourge, and fire; that can sustain the long discipline by which the mean and false and evil elements are driven out of the beloved soul. But such is the love of God. "The grace of God hath appeared, bringing salvation to all men, instructing us" (disciplining us, Titus 2:12, R.V.). So it came to Jacob.

If we had been asked to tell which of these two men was Heaven's favorite, we should, in all likelihood, have selected the wrong one.

Here stands Esau, the shaggy, broad-shouldered, red-haired huntsman, equipped with bow and arrows, full of generous impulse, affectionate to his aged father, forgiving to the brother who had done him such grievous wrong. He became a chieftain of renown, and the ancestor of a princely line (Gen. 36). He was happy in his wives and children; we read of no such outbreaks as embittered Jacob's lot. He was so rich that he could make light of Jacob's presents; and so powerful that Jacob's company was helpless in his hand. His people were happily settled in their rich territories; while the children of Jacob were groaning in Egyptian bondage. And, as we consider him, we are inclined to imitate the words of Samuel, when Jesse's eldest son entered his presence, and say: "Surely, the Lord's anointed is before Him!"

There, on the other hand, is Jacob. In his young manhood, an exile from his father's house. In his mature manhood, a hireling, in the employ of a kinsman. In his declining years, worn by anxiety and trouble. In his old age, a stranger in a strange land. Few and evil were the days of the years of his pilgrimage. Yet *he* was the beloved of God; and it was because of that especial love that he was exposed to such searching discipline. "Whom the Lord loveth He chasteneth, and scourgeth every son whom He receiveth" (Heb. 12:6).

Earthly prosperity is no sign of the special love of Heaven; nor are sorrow and care any mark of God's disfavor, but the reverse. "Jesus loved Martha, and her sister, and Lazarus. When He had heard, therefore, that he was sick, He abode where He was," and let Lazarus die. God's love is robust, and true, and eager—not for our comfort, but for our lasting blessedness; it is bent on achieving this, and it is strong enough to bear misrepresentation and rebuke in its attempts to attune our spirits to higher music. It therefore comes instructing us.

Let us enter ourselves as pupils in the school of God's love. Let us lay aside our own notions of the course of study; let us submit ourselves to be led and taught; let us be prepared for any lessons that may be given from the blackboard of sorrow; let us be so assured of the inexhaustible tenacity of His love, as to dare to trust Him, though He slay us. And let us look forward to that august moment when He will give us a reason for all life's discipline, with a smile that shall thrill our souls with ecstasy, and constrain sorrow and sighing to flee away forever.

IV. JACOB'S LIFE GIVES A CLUE TO THE DOCTRINE OF ELECTION. There was election here. The Apostle Paul uses it to illustrate that mysterious truth (Rom. 9:11). And it is obviously so. Jacob was the younger son; and his life is as much a Gospel for younger sons as is that matchless parable of the prodigal. The children were not born when God foretold and fixed their destiny.

It is impossible to ignore election; it has been truly said to the be the key to the order of all nature and history. "There are elect angels; elect stars; elect races of animals; elect flowers and fruits; elect human souls. Nowhere do we meet with equality, uniformity, the monotony of a dull level. Everywhere things and beings, with superior endowment to other things and beings, seem made to head them, and sweep them along in the orbit of their motion by the attraction of the superior on the inferior spheres. One star differs from another star in glory; some flash forth resplendent, regal gems in the diadem of night, while others are scattered faint and dim like seed pearls on her dusky robe."

So is it with souls. Some men are evidently born to be the leaders, teachers, masters of mankind. Thus it was with Jeremiah the prophet (Jer. 1:5); with Cyrus the conqueror (Is. 45:1, 4); and John the Baptist (Luke 1:17)—and these are types of myriads more.

But to what are these elect? To comfort, ease, success? Nay, for these things fall to the lot rather of the Esaus than the Jacobs. The elect of God seem chosen to stand in the front rank, and bear the brunt of the storms of sorrow, pain, and care.

Are they, then, elect to personal salvation? Many of the cases in which the words occur do not demand this as their exclusive meaning. Indeed, Scripture does not certainly exclude Esau himself from a share in Abraham's bosom. He lost his birthright, truly, and he could not recover it by strong cryings and tears, but the loss of his birthright did not necessarily entail the loss of his soul.

But may we not hold that election refers largely, if not primarily, to the *service* which the elect are qualified to render to their fellows throughout all coming time? They are elect, not for themselves, or for the sake of their own future, but rather for the sake of the work which their position of privilege may enable them to do for mankind.

This, certainly, has been one result of the election of Jacob and his people. They were elect to be the spiritual leaders and teachers of mankind; to furnish us with a matchless religious literature; to provide a suitable platform on which the Savior of the world should appear, and from which He might influence the world. Not for the sake of their own comfort, but for the sake of the dark and dying world, God gave them light and life, and sustained them in existence against overwhelming odds, and stored in them streams of electric force, as in some mighty battery.

This, then, will explain also the terrific discipline through which they passed. It was needed, not for their sakes alone, but also for the race they were destined to serve; that they might be set free from deteriorating influences, and stand forth as God's chosen vessels, brimming with blessing for the world.

Seeking souls need not then concern themselves with this mysterious subject. Outside the house of salvation, there is no word but this— "whosoever." When once we have crossed the threshold and looked around, we may find some such text as that with which Peter begins his first epistle; and we may find that God had some purpose of mercy to others, when He first drew us to Himself.

But his and many other similar questions will receive new and beautiful illustrations, as we pursue our studies of Jacob's life.

2

The Sale of the Birthright

We shape ourselves the joy or fear
Of which the coming life is made;
And fill our future's atmosphere
With sunshine or with shade.
The tissue of the life to be
We weave with colors all our own;
And in the fields of Destiny
We reap as we have sown.
Whittier

Genesis 25

Brothers were these two men, yes, twin brothers, but brothers could not differ more widely. Before their birth their difference was foretold. At their birth it was evident. From their birth it began to broaden and increase. The linked hands of the brothers, reaching across the tiny rill of their earliest infancy, were soon parted, as the stream of life widened between them, and they passed to their destiny along the opposite banks.

They differed in appearance. Esau was rough, ruddy, and hairy. He would give the impression of great bodily strength; capacity for vast physical fatigue; and a temperament which would incline him to exciting and hazardous pursuits. Jacob was the reverse: smooth in skin; dark in feature; slight in build; no match for his burly brother in physical force, but more than his match in guile.

They differed in pursuits. Esau was a cunning hunter, a man of the field and chase. Had he been living now, he would have been foremost in all manly, daring, outdoor sports. Nor would it be difficult to find his duplicate today among our high-born youth: with handsome face, generous disposition, and open hand; quick to resent, and quick to forgive; perfect in dress; polished in manner; a rare shot, a splendid rider, an expert in all manly exercise; and certain to marry well—as Esau did—and found a strong and noble house. Jacob, on the other hand, loved the home life. The violent exercise and hazards for which Esau pined, as an imprisoned eagle for its rocky, storm-beaten crags, had no fascination for him. And while Esau was away, he was content to dwell among the flocks and herds of the camp; content with the peaceful occupations of an uneventful pastoral life. Each man to his taste!

They differed most in character. There is much in Esau which makes us like him; and we should have been certainly more quickly attracted to him than to his brother. If he was impetuous, he was generous. If he was rash, he was frank. If he was singularly wanting in religious fervor, he was a good son. If his heart doted on the pleasures of the chase, he was splendid company, and every inch a man. But, for all this, he was decidedly sensual—Scripture calls him *profane*—i.e., he was a slave to his senses; he hailed anything that would thrill him with pleasant though transient excitement; he was willing to purchase pleasure at any price, though he had to pawn the most priceless jewels of his spirit; he was, indeed, too enamored with the claims of the passing hour to care for unseen realities; or to seek the eternal harvest which lies beyond the bitter sowing times of patience, and waiting, and pain. Alas, that he should have had such a host of imitators!

Jacob was a "plain" man (a 'quiet' man, R.V. *marg.*), but under that calm exterior there were depths and depths. Amid all the craft and duplicity of his nature, there was immense capacity for religious fervor and religious faith. He could understand, as Esau never could, the meaning of the birthright, with all its spiritual glow and glory. He could draw aside the veil of the unseen, and weigh its promises, and compare its treasures with the shows of earth. He could dream angel-haunted dreams, that threw a mystic ladder over the abyss of space, linking all worlds. And while Esau was occupied with pleasure, Jacob would feel within him the strange stirrings of a nature which could not be satisfied with anything within the narrow limits of his tents, but which yearned for that spiritual heritage which was summed up in the word "birthright."

Let us consider—the Birthright; the Barter; and the Bitter Cry.

I. THE BIRTHRIGHT. What was it? It was not worldly prosperity; for though Esau lost it, he had an abundant fortune: four hundred armed retainers followed at his heel; the great country of Edom owned his sway; till, after a life of splendid and unbroken prosperity, he went down to the grave in peace and a good old age. There is nothing in the brief record which we have of him to make us think that he lived a broken or disappointed life. All that this world could give was his. The sunshine of worldly prosperity touched with golden light all the wavelets that broke upon the beach of his life. The exceeding bitter wail of momentary disappointment was soon forgotten in his satisfaction at having lost nothing which he really cared for, while so much was still left to him that his soul loved. Whatever the birthright was, it evidently was not worldly prosperity; for of this, Esau, who lost it, probably had more than Jacob, who won it.

It was not immunity from sorrow. When Jacob had secured it, it seemed as if the mystic box of Pandora had been opened in his home; for every human ill was let free into his life. Staff in hand, he tears himself from home, and seeks a distant country. A hireling in a kinsman's house, he spends the best years of manhood's prime. Halting on his thigh, he bows before Esau; buries his favorite Rachel; chafes over the open sores of his home life; is bereaved of his children; and moans that the days of the years of his pilgrimage have been evil and few. Few have trodden a more rugged path, or bound about their brows a crown more set with thorns. It was a sad and weary life that breathed itself out in that hieroglyphed chamber in the land of the Pharaohs, when for the last time he gathered his feet into his bed, and was gathered unto his people. Whatever the birthright was, it evidently was not freedom from pain and grief; for of these, Jacob, who won it, had infinitely more than Esau, who lost it.

The birthright was a spiritual heritage. It gave the right—which ever belonged to its possessor—of being the priest of the family or clan. It carried the privilege of being the depository and communicator of the Divine secrets. It constituted a link in the line of descent by which the Messiah was to be born into the world. The right of wielding power with God and men; the right of catching up and handing on—as in the old Greek race—the torch of Messianic hope; the right of heirship to the promises of the covenant made to Abraham; the right of standing among the spiritual aristocracy of mankind; the right of being a pilgrim of eternity, owning no foot of earth, because all heaven was held in fee—this, and more than this, was summed up in the possession of the birthright.

It was a fair heritage, but a fairer one is the birthright of every reader of these lines. You have been born into a world which has been trodden by the feet and wet by the tears of the Son of God. You have been born of a race whose redemption has been purchased at the exceeding great price of His precious blood. You have been born of a nature which has been taken up by Him, who passed by that of angels. And such a birth carries with it rights, given by the matchless grace of God, which as much outshine the birthrights of the old world, as the regalia of England does the crown of Alfred.

Your birth gives you the right to be translated from the kingdom of darkness into the kingdom of God's dear Son; the right to claim of the Holy Ghost the second birth; the right to be forgiven and saved; the right to become the sons and daughters of the Lord God Almighty; the right to stand side by side with the Son in His glory, joint heirs with Him of all that is His; the right to be more than conquerors over all the power of our foes; the right to be delivered from sin, and to join the jubilant throng that stands on the shores of the sea of glass mingled with fire.

This may be your glorious heritage. It cannot be purchased, or won by might of arm. It is reserved for those only who, having been born of woman, have also been born of the Holy Ghost. It may be amid tears and storm that the heart will first realize its right to participate in this inheritance; yet, even then, the thought and hope of its future heritage will cheer the spirit when passing through the stern discipline of life, on its way to the promised rest. That hope shall not be shamed. And surely it will be the standing marvel of eternity that a destiny so bright was ever put within the reach of the fallen children of this sin-cursed earth.

II. THE BARTER. One day Jacob was standing over a caldron of savory pottage, made of those red lentils which to the present day form a dish highly relished in Syria and in Egypt. The appetizing odor soon filled the air, enticing enough for a full, to say nothing of a hungry man. At that moment, who should come in but Esau, faint with hunger. He did not know the name: his active life left him little time for such trifles as domestic cookery, but the sight and smell were quite enough to convince him that Jacob's preparations would be marvelously suitable to stay the cravings of his hunter's hunger. "Give me some of that red— that red," he cried impatiently.

Now Jacob was not wholly a selfish man, but it suddenly occurred to him that this would be a good opportunity of winning the right to be the spiritual leader of the clan. So, knowing well how little his brother counted on his rights, he made the extraordinary proposal to exchange the mess of pottage for the birthright.

Esau closed with the proposal. "Behold," said the bluff hunter, "I am on the point to die; and what profit shall this birthright do to me?" On the one hand was the birthright—a myth, so far as he could see, a vision of the far future, wholly unseen and spiritual. On the other hand was this pottage, right before him, and very tempting to his hunger. So he made over his birthright to Jacob. And Jacob gave him bread and pottage of lentils; and he did eat and drink, and went his way—not, I think, without some qualms of conscience: and thus Esau despised his birthright.

We cannot exonerate either of these men from blame. Jacob was not only a traitor to his brother, but he was faithless towards his God. Had it not been distinctly whispered in his mother's ear that the elder of the brothers should serve the younger? Had not the realization of his loftiest ambition been pledged by One whose faithfulness had been the theme of repeated talks with Abraham, who had survived during the first eighteen years of his young life? He might have been well assured that what the God of Abraham had promised He was able also to perform; and would perform, without the aid of his own miserable schemes. But how hard is it for us to quietly wait for God! We are too apt to outrun Him; to forestall the quiet unfolding of His purposes; and to snatch at promised blessings before they are ripe.

And as for Esau, we can never forget the beacon words of Scripture: "Look diligently, lest there be any profane person, as Esau, who for one morsel of meat sold his birthright" (Heb. 12:6). Yet let us, in condemning him across the ages, look close at home. How many are there among ourselves, born into the world with splendid talents; dowried with unusual powers; inheritors of noble names; heirs to vast estates; gifted with keys to unlock any of the many doors to name, and fame, and usefulness—who yet fling away all these possibilities of blessing and blessedness, for one brief plunge into the Stygian pool of selfish and sensual indulgence!

The strongest and bravest men in build and muscle are often the weakest in resisting the appeals of momentary passion. Esau is mastered by the fragrance of a mess of pottage; Samson by the charms of a Philistine girl; Peter by the question of a servant. There is no strength apart from the strong Son of God.

And the appeals to sense come most often when we are least expecting them. When we say, Peace and safety, then sudden destruction comes. The foe creeps through the postern gate. The arrow penetrates the joints of the harness. The moment of crisis is the moment when we come in from the dangers of the chase to the home which promised us immunity from the attack. "Watch ye, therefore, and pray always; that ye may be accounted worthy to escape all these things."

These appeals, moreover, come in the most trivial things. One mess of pottage; one glass of drink; one moment's unbridled passion; one afternoon's saunter; a question and an answer; a movement or a look. It is in such small things—small as the angle at which railway lines diverge from each other to east and west—that great alternatives are offered and great decisions made. When we fail in some such thing, we often comfort ourselves with the reflection that we could and would do right in some all-important crisis. We cannot pray in a bedroom, but we could burn at a stake. We cannot speak to an individual, but we could preach at a Pentecost. We little understand ourselves. We do not see that trifles are the truest test of character; and that if we cannot run with footmen, we certainly could not contend with horses; and if we have been wearied in the land of peace, we certainly shall stand no chance when we are called to battle with the swellings of Jordan. There are no trifles in Christian living. Everything is great, because the mightiest events revolve on the smallest pivots; and the greatest harvests for good and ill spring from the tiniest seeds.

Had we been at Esau's side, how eagerly should we have laid our hand upon his shoulder, entreating him to pause and consider, before he bartered the spiritual for the physical; the eternal for the temporal; the unseen for the seen. "Will it pay?" "Is it wise?" "Will you get an equivalent for that which you forfeit now forever?" And such questions are asked still of all Esaus who are tempted to barter their peace, their manhood, their heaven, for one mess of the devil's pottage. It steams. It smells savory. It promises to do more good to you than all the Bible put together. The tempter whispers, "Thou shalt not surely die. Bow down and worship me, and all shall be thine. Give me that which thou hast; and I will give thee this and much more." Then it is that a still small voice asks, "What shall it profit a man if he gain the world and lose himself? How much less will it profit him to lose his all for one small mess of pottage, which will only secure a brief respite from the cravings of appetite." Learn to master appetite in Christ's strength; this will serve thee better far than warding off its urgency for a time, leaving it to return with whetted hunger, like a pack of wolves which have tasted blood. "Hold that fast which thou hast, that no man take thy crown."

III. THE BITTER CRY. When Esau saw that God had taken him at his word, and had taken away from him the birthright of spiritual primacy, "he cried with an exceeding great and bitter cry" (Gen. 28:34, R.V.). But that cry came too late to alter the consequences of his rash act. "He found no place of repentance" (no way to change his father's decision), "though he sought it carefully with tears."

"No place of repentance!" On many hearts those words have rung the knell of hope. As the heartbroken sinner has reviewed a blighted past with bitter tears and cries, the adversary of souls has whispered that he has sinned too deeply for repentance, and wandered too far to return; and he has backed the insinuation with these terrible words— *"no place of repentance."*

And is it so? Is it possible for a soul, on this side of death, to reach a position where tears and prayers will strike against the brazen heavens, and rebound, only an echo? It cannot be. It is possible that a man should become too callous and hard to desire salvation: *this* is the sin unto death; *this* is the sin that hath never forgiveness; and it has no forgiveness because the sinner does not desire or seek it. But it is impossible for a man to desire to repent and not find a ready help in the grace of the Holy Ghost. It is impossible for a man to seek forgiveness with bitter tears, and not obtain it. It is impossible for a man to knock at the door of mercy, and not find it open at last, though after long delay: "All manner of sin and blasphemy shall be forgiven unto me." In point of fact, these desires and tears and prayers are blessed symptoms that the work of grace and forgiveness has begun within the soul. They are not of man; or of the will of the flesh: but of God. And when God puts His hand to the plow in a human spirit, He never looks back.

But the "repentance" mentioned here is not repentance to salvation, but the power of reversing the past. Esau could not undo what he had done. He had long despised his birthright. That act of surrender was not a solitary one, but the outcome of a state of heart. It simply revealed thoughts that had been long admitted guests in the inner chamber of his being. But when once this temper had taken effect in a definite promise, asseverated by an oath, God held him to it—yea, nature and righteousness and conscience held him to it too; and he could not alter it by his tears or bitter cries.

The sinful past is irrevocable. Eve might bitterly regret her choice, but as she stood with Adam outside the cherub-guarded gate, with the faded rose in her hand—of which Rabbis tell us—her bitter regrets could not replace the apple on the tree, or reinstate her within the golden bowers of Paradise. Peter went out and wept bitterly, but those tears of uncontrollable anguish could not recall the words of denial, or blot from his memory that look of pain. The Virgins might beat their breasts in bitter self-reproach, but no complaints, however pitiable, could reverse the decision of the Bridegroom's lips.

We all know this. We remember bursts of passion which have broken hearts; sundered ties of love; clouded sunny skies; withered hopes; and shattered promising prospects. We would give worlds to blot out the record, and to make them as if they had never been. But it is impossible. We cannot bring back the shadow on the dial. We cannot reverse the writing of the faithful chronicler. We cannot find a chance for altering the decisions, which had been long floating in solution in our minds, but which have had one fatal and irrevocable crystallization in word or act. There is no place of repentance, though we seek it carefully and with tears. You cannot undo.

But though the past is irrevocable, it is not irreparable. In the garden of Gethsemane our Lord said mournfully to the chosen three, "Sleep on now, and take your rest," but He instantly added, "Arise: let us be going." In the first sentence, He taught the irrevocableness of the past; they might as well sleep, for any good that watching could now do. But in the second sentence, he taught that there was still a future before them, with new chances, and opportunities, and hopes.

So shall it ever be. God Himself cannot undo the past. But He can and will forgive. He will not mention the past, but give us a fair, fresh start. He will even "restore the years that the cankerworm has eaten." He will give us new opportunities of showing how truly we repent the decisions of the past; and how loyally we desire to serve Him in the decisions of the future. He will not even mention the thrice denial, but He will give us three opportunities of saying how much we love Him, as He thrice bids us tend His flock. "The King is dead!"—that is the proclamation of the irrevocable past. "Long live the King!"—that is the announcement of an available future.

3

The Stolen Blessing

No action, whether foul or fair,
Is ever done, but it leaves somewhere
A record, written by fingers ghostly
As a blessing, or a curse; and mostly
In the greater weakness or greater strength
Of the acts which follow it: till at length
The wrongs of ages are redressed
And the justice of God made manifest.
Anonymous

Genesis 25

I n many a picturesque English village there lies a pond of stagnant water, which has been there as long as the oldest inhabitant can remember. It looks innocent enough when the winds of March sweep it, or the leaves of October bestrew it, but when it is exposed to the scorching rays of a summer sun, it pours forth volumes of poisonous gases, which had lurked unnoticed in its depths, and typhoid fever is sown in the homes that cluster round. Such is the heart of man. We do not think, we do not care to know, how much evil lies within. We read with listless interest the terrible photograph given by One who could not exaggerate (Mark 7:21); and attach a vague meaning to other words which characterize the human heart as "desperately wicked." And yet we do not feel so bad; nor shall we truly verify those words; nor realize how evil our nature is; or what a dying need we have for God—until we have been exposed to some searching test, which shall reveal us to ourselves.

Temptation is such a test. There is no sin in being tempted. Our great High Priest was "tempted in all points like as we are, yet without sin." And temptation need not necessarily lead to sin; so long as the steadfast will, inspired by the Holy Spirit, keeps the door of the nature shut and locked. Nay, temptation is even a blessing: "Blessed is the man that endureth temptation," when it leads a man to discover tendencies, movement, appetites within him—unknown before, but against which he must henceforth be on his guard.

God our Father permits us to be tempted, to lead us to see the hidden evils of our heart—to hold up a looking glass before us, in which we may behold what manner of people we are; and to make us so sensible of our own worthlessness and deformity as to drive us to hand ourselves over to Him, to do anything He may please, if only we may be delivered out of this body of death. To know oneself, and to despair of oneself, is to come within the sweep of that gracious power, which can fashion a temple column out of a bruised reed; and a noble vessel out of a lump of clay; and an Israel out of a Jacob.

We need not be at all astonished, then, to learn that temptation was allowed to come to Jacob from an unexpected source, taking him unawares. And if you are truly desirous of ascending the higher reaches of Christian thought and life, you must not be astonished if, in answer to your prayer for more grace and life, your heavenly Lover should take some unexpected means of showing you what you are. So Newton found—

> I asked the Lord that I might grow
> In faith, and love, and every grace;
> Might more of His salvation know,
> And see the glory of His face.
>
> Instead of this, He made me feel
> The hidden evils of my heart;
> And let the angry powers of hell
> Assault my soul in every part.

I. THE TEMPTATION ORIGINATED IN A SENSUOUS REQUEST OF ISAAC. We sometimes find it hard to think that the Isaac of this chapter is the same person as the submissive boy who carried the altar wood on his stalwart young shoulders, and wondered about the lamb, and meekly submitted to be bound as a sacrifice. That was a radiant dawn for a human life, which for some reason became quickly overcast.

What was that reason? Was it the prosperity of which we read in the previous chapter? "The man waxed great, and went forward, and grew until he became very great." It would not be the last time that prosperity has choked off spiritual growth. Was it a too-easy disposition, of which we catch a glimpse in his readiness to abandon well after well, if only he might be left in peace? It would not be the only time that a molluscous lack of backbone has barred the path of a noble career. Was it an inordinate love for the pleasures of the table? There seems to have been too much of this in his constitution. He said to Esau, "Make me savory meat, such as I love." Rebekah was keenly aware of her husband's weakness in this respect: "I will make for thy father savory meat such as he loveth." There is a sad suggestiveness in all this, and enough to account for all. The man who, on the supposed point of death, thinks most of all of a good dish of delicious venison, is not likely to shine as a specially brilliant star in the heavenly firmament.

We need to take warning against the twin sins of gluttony and drunkenness. Intemperance in eating may not result in the same outward degradation as in drinking, but it is as harmful to the spirit. The question is, whether average Christian people do not eat much more than is good for the health of either body or spirit. Certainly the world and the Church are filled with numberless cases of men, the brilliance of whose minds has been obscured, and the edge of their spiritual life blunted, by their habitual and greedy indulgence in superfluous and luxurious food. With every grace we say at our meals, we need to ask that we may eat and drink, not merely at our own caprice, but to the glory of God. "Take heed to yourselves, lest at any time your hearts be overcharged with *surfeiting*, and drunkenness, and cares."

Many years had passed since that memorable day on Mount Moriah; and many signs told Isaac that his sun was setting. Chief among these was dimming sight. God has mercifully arranged that such reminders, like warning bells, should ring out to show us how far we have traveled, and how near we are to the terminus of life. Many a man, who otherwise had dropped carelessly into the grave, has been awakened by such things to say to himself, "Behold, now I am old; I know not the day of my death. I must begin to prepare for the final act."

There are glimpses of the better things in Isaac's character in the threefold preparation he made for his end.

He made his last testamentary disposition. If you have not done this, do it at once—no time is so good as this. Leave nothing uncertain; nothing to chance; no loophole for heart burning or heartbreak among your heirs. *He laid aside his earthly cares.* He lived for several years after this, but he was a man set apart. It was the gloaming of his life; not quite dark, yet not light enough to work—the fittest time for meditation and prayer. It was ever the ambition of Dr. Chalmers to have such a time of Sabbath calm after the busy rush of his life of working days, and before the final act. *He handed on the blessing.* Even though he proposed to counterwork the purposes of God, yet there is a significant beauty in the desire of the old man to bless before he died. Aged people, we younger ones have surely a right to expect some blessing, ere you leave us, of ripe counsel; of matured wisdom; of prophetic experience.

II. THIS TEMPTATION WAS PRESENTED TO JACOB THROUGH THE UNSCRUPULOUS LOVE OF REBEKAH. Jacob was her favorite son. There was a closer relationship between them than there could be between her and the more random Esau. As soon as she overheard Isaac's request to Esau, she resolved at once to win his blessing for her younger boy. And if a momentary qualm suggested itself, she, doubtless, quieted it by the reflection that she was simply trying to ratify the bargain which he had made for himself.

We cannot but admire her love. She threw herself away on this lad, whom she was never to see again. She was reckless of personal consequences. She cared not what might come to herself, so that he might win. "Upon me be thy curse, my son." For him she sacrificed husband, elder son, principle—*all.* It is with such prodigality of affection that women constantly give themselves for their beloved. Their love is often worthy of a better object; and yet it is beautiful. Oh that all such knew of Him on whom the saint of the home at Bethany, and the sinner in the house of Simon, broke their alabaster boxes in a very prodigality of love, and yet there was no waste!

But Rebekah's love was not based on principle. And such love is as terrible as the fire which has burst from the restraints of iron bars, and leaves behind it a scorched and blackened trail. Love is either the bliss or bane of life: it is bliss, if rooted and grounded in an all-mastering and all-penetrating devotion to purity, truth, principle—or in a word, to God, but it is curse, if, like some pirate crew, it steers the ship of life according to its own wild whim. Let us keep our hearts above all that we guard, since out of them are the issues of life. And if we are ever prompted to act according to the strong solicitation of mere natural affection, let us remember the havoc which such a course produced in that far-off Eastern home, under the black tents of the patriarch Isaac: how it deceived the husband; wronged the elder son; drove the younger to an enforced exile; and blasted the reputation of this woman, who otherwise had been honored and beloved.

But Rebekah is not the only mother who has acted thus. As we review her life, we find its counterpart in many: who will scheme, maneuver, palter with truth and righteousness, and cast even conjugal love into the scale, if only, at all hazards, they can advance the interests of their child. How little do they realize the harvest of which these are the seeds—a harvest of misery for the home; of heart burning and hatred; of sorrow for those whom they would benefit; and of heartbreaking anguish for themselves.

In another sense than our Savior meant, a man's foes may be they of his own household. We exert a vast influence—not only by what we say, but by the spirit of our lives—on those who dwell under the same roof, and address us by the tenderest names. And, alas! this influence is often sadly averse to their nobler life, withering it, as gas does flowers. They see us in our most careless moments, when we have ungirded ourselves, and lie at ease on the grass. They catch up our least guarded words. They take us at a disadvantage, when, biased by love, we try to solve their problems and answer their questions so as to make life's pathway as easy as possible for their feet. And one drop of poison instilled into the heart by a loved and trusted friend is enough to spoil a life. We drink more unquestioningly of the poisoned chalice, when put to our lips by one we love. We enter more unsuspectingly the pathway to ruin, when the hand of parent or friend points the way. The course of deceit is less forbidding, when urged on us by those who, like Rebekah, can gain nothing if we succeed; who are willing to assume all responsibility if we fail; and who profess that they are inspired by no other motive than the most unselfish devotion to our interests.

How careful should we be, then, of all suggestions and advice we give to those accustomed to look up to us; lest, wittingly or not, we should place a stumblingblock and occasion to fall in another's way. In such matters affection is no true guide, unless regulated, as God's is, by the dictates of righteousness and truth; if these be absent, there is terrible danger lest we should make again the mistake of Rebekah, and follow again in the footsteps of her sin, against her sons, herself, and her God.

III. THIS TEMPTATION WAS GREEDILY RESPONDED TO BY THE WEAK AND CRAFTY NATURE OF JACOB. Jacob was not a thoroughly vicious man, but he was deplorably weak: and weakness is close akin to the sin to which it inevitably leads. He would not have concocted this plot or laid the train himself. He would have preferred not to act the liar. He was really afraid of the result. But he had not the courage to say "No" to the strong will and wish of his mother, especially when she was ready to take all risks. He tried to quiet his conscience by the consideration that he was only trying to get his own; and that Esau had no right to think of getting back from their father the birthright which he had certainly sold. And so, when his mother put strong pressure on him, summoning him by the obedience he owed her as her son (v. 8), he weakly did not refuse on the ground that it was unlawful, but suggested it was inexpedient, lest they should be found out. "Behold, Esau my brother is a hairy man, and I am a smooth man; my father peradventure will feel me, and I shall seem to him as a deceiver, and I shall bring a curse upon me, and not a blessing." When a man retreats from the position of what is right, to the urging of what is likely to be expedient and to pay—that man is near a fall, swift as the archangel's from heaven to hell.

Such a fall was Jacob's. It is impossible to emphasize this point too earnestly, especially for the young. So long as we take our stand on what is lawful—as John the Baptist did, when he strode into the royal pres-

ence and told Herod that he had *no right* to take his brother's wife—
we are impregnable. But when once we retreat from this, and argue
with the tempter on the lower grounds of possible discovery and failure, we shall find ourselves outmatched by his arithmetic, and led as
garlanded oxen to the slaughterhouse. Into this fault, to which all weak
men are so liable, Jacob fell; and so, when, a second time, his mother
commanded him to obey her voice (v. 13), and go to the flock for two
good kids of the goats, "he went, and fetched, and brought them to his
mother."

When once the first step had been taken, it was quickly followed by
others which it seemed to render needful. Sin never comes alone. The
first act of sin is like the boy put through a narrow window into a
burglar-beset house, who creeps round to pen the door for the entire
gang; or it is like the first link of the rusty chain, which draws all the rest
into the hold of the ship. If the graces come with linked hands, so do
the vices. They are sporadic. That first sin of Jacob led to many others.

He simulated his brother's dress and skin. While the meat was
cooking, Rebekah was engaged in turning over Esau's wardrobe, to
find some suitable garments, highly perfumed, as is the custom with the
Easterns to this day. This done, she prepared the delicate skins of the
kids for his hands and neck. All was done with haste; lest Esau might
come in. And when all was ready, Jacob arrayed himself to play his part.

He deceived his father with a direct falsehood. "I am Esau, thy
firstborn; I have done according as thou badest me; eat of my venison,
that thy soul may bless me."

He made an impious use of the name of God. In answer to Isaac's
question as to how he had found it so quickly, he dared to say, "The
Lord thy God brought it to me."

Yet what horror must have thrilled him as he found himself forced
to take step after step, aware that he was being carried out by a rushing stream towards an ocean of ink; yet not daring to stop—nay, compelled to press still further out to sea. How his heart must have stood
still when the old man became suspicious, and doubted his voice, and
insisted on feeling, smelling, and having him near! What if God should
strike him dead! What a relief when he came out again in the fresh air,
though the words of the coveted blessing hardly repaid him for the

agony he had passed through! How he must have loathed himself, and longed to change places with the lizards that crept about the tents, or the little naked slave children that laughed so merrily at play! The sun itself seemed shorn of half its light.

Yet this is the man who became the Prince of God. And if he became so, is there not hope for us, who can trace in him many resemblances to ourselves? "Though we have lien among the pots, yet may we be as the wings of a dove, covered with yellow gold." If the Almighty Workman could fashion such clay into so fair a vessel, what may He not do for us? Our only hope is to hand ourselves over to Him, in an act of entire self-surrender; conscious that we are useless and worthless, deserving rather to be trampled under foot than fashioned by his hand; conscious, too, that if He do not work for us, we are undone; willing to be and do anything He may direct; careful to work *out* all that He may work *in*. If only we will to do this, and yield ourselves to God, and be willing to be made willing to have his will done in us, by us, and about us, then God will be able to work in us also some fair design of beauty and use. Oh, do not mar His work; or lead Him to make of thee some inferior vessel to that which thou mayest become! (Jer. 18:4).

But, remember, God must implant the nature which He educates into Israel the Prince. When we speak of God's education, we must be very careful what we mean, and how we express it; lest we should countenance error. Amidst all his sin, there must have been in Jacob a better self, which was capable of receiving the education of God, and of being developed into Israel. You may call this *faith*, or what you will, but it was there. And it was the possession of this better nature that made Jacob stand in a different relation towards God than Esau did; and made him capable of rising to a spiritual level, for which Esau had neither the aptitude nor the taste.

No doubt the God of love had thoughts of love towards Esau, but there was not, in his worldly nature, the faith, or the elements of nobility, which, through faith, had been implanted in his brother's heart. Put a stone into a flowerpot; cover it with mold; give it water and sunshine, and light and air—it will always be a stone: so if Esau had passed through the discipline of Jacob, he would always have been an Esau—he never could have been an Israel; unless there had been also in him the better nature which is associated with faith. You may develop intelligence, by education and mind culture, but the faculty must be already present, otherwise your best methods will be abortive. You can develop the rudimentary germ, but when it is absent, you cannot create it. So the discipline of God's grace in a human life can do nothing, unless there be the germ of that new and divine nature of which our Lord spoke to Nicodemus: "That which is born of the flesh is flesh; that which is born of the Spirit is spirit. Ye must be born again."

If, then, you are conscious of a depraved nature, capable of the faults which disfigure the character of Jacob, be anxious to inquire if, besides this, there is the new nature, born of God, and capable of being educated into His image. If it be there, be thankful; and ask the Holy Spirit to lust against and repress the Jacob-nature, so that you may not do the things that you would (Gal. 5:17, R.V.), and to hasten your Israel-beauty. If it be not there, your duty is to look at once to the Lamb of God, who was delivered for your sins, and was raised again for your justification; and the imparting, by the Holy Ghost, of the germ of the new and better nature will be simultaneous with the first real longing, transforming look of faith to the Lord Jesus.

4

The Angel Ladder

Though like the wanderer,
Daylight all gone,
Darkness be over me,
My rest a stone:
Yet, in my dreams, I'd be
Nearer, my God, to Thee,
Nearer to Thee
S. F. Adams

Genesis 28

When Esau found that Jacob had stolen his blessing, he hated him, and vowed to kill him. This was nothing less than might have been expected from his headstrong and impetuous nature. These threats came to Rebekah's ears, and filled her with fear, lest she should be deprived of them both in one day—Jacob, the jewel of her eye, by the hand of his brother; and Esau, by being compelled, like a second Cain, to become an outlaw for his brother's murder.

But there was one source of relief which presented itself to her mother's love and woman's wit. She understood Esau's temperament perfectly. She knew that a passionate, hasty man is less to be feared than a man who gives no sign of the tumult raging within. Rage like Esau's would soon expend itself in words and threats and burn itself out, like a quick and furious fire, for want of fuel. If only Jacob absented himself for a short time, all would be forgotten. So Rebekah made up her mind that he should go across the desert to Haran; to abide for a time with her brother Laban, from whom she had been parted since that memorable day, when, with many a girlish dream floating before her dark eyes, she had started with Abraham's servant for her new home. She did not tell her husband all her reasons—it would have done more harm than good, but she adduced very good and obvious ones, in the necessity of preserving from defilement the holy seed, and of procuring for Jacob a suitable wife.

Isaac fell in with the proposal; and "called Jacob, and blessed him, and charged him, and said unto him, Thou shalt not take a wife of the daughters of Canaan. Arise, go to Padam-aram; and take thee a wife of the daughters of Laban, thy mother's brother. And God Almighty bless thee!" And Jacob, not without many a tear, went out from Beersheba, and went toward Haran. And it was on his way that this revelation of the Angel-Ladder was made to him.

I. THE CIRCUMCISION IN WHICH THIS REVELATION WAS MADE TO HIM. Jacob was lonely. He was not what we should call a young man; he had reached mature years: but it is almost certain that this was the first time of his leaving the shelter of his home. Led far from home in pursuit of the fleet deer, his hunter brother may often have passed the night amid the wilds, comfortable and content. But Jacob had no taste for such experiences. For him solitude had no charms; he loved to hear the sounds of human voices, and the stir of the camp. In the early morning light, as he started forth there may have been an exhilarating sense of independence, freshness, and novelty, but as night drew its curtains over the world, and the stars glimmered out of the depths, and the solemn boulders lay so still on the moorland around him—with no tent for shelter, no fire form warmth, no pillow for rest, there stole over his mind a sense of loneliness and melancholy. This was God's chosen time, when He drew near to his spirit, and said, "Behold, I am with thee; and will keep thee in all places whither thou goest; and will bring thee again into this land: for I will not leave thee, until I have done that which I have spoken to thee of." And so it has often been with men. We must be withdrawn from the rush and hum of the busy marketplace, if in the old minister we would see the calm angel faces carved in stone, or hear the thrilling notes of the chorister boys. Recall, for a moment, your first night away from home—as a schoolboy; or apprentice; or servant; or student: and answer, if that were not a sacred epoch in your history, when God took up the trailing tendrils of your love, and twined them around Himself, and you realized His presence, and clung to Him as never before.

Jacob was also standing on the threshold of independence. It is a solemn moment when a man enters on independence—fairly afloat like a swimmer without forks; adrift like a boat's crew who have seen the waves close over their ship. Childhood sleeps peacefully, because it has no responsibilities; the flower is sheathed in its green case; the nestling is fed and shielded by the untiring care of the parent bird. But this does not last long; and none need wish prematurely to exchange such dependence for the independence that must needs care for itself. The child must go forth at last to earn his own living; to win his spurs; to stand alone; to choose and act for himself. It is a solemn crisis.

But it is at such a moment that the Almighty, as a wayfaring man, offers His company for the untrodden path. Happy is he who accepts the proffered help; and transfers the feeling of dependence from the earthly to the heavenly Friend. It is almost worthwhile being cast off by father and mother, if one may be taken up by the Lord. And when one is willing to be taken up by Him, there need be no further anxiety or care; for directly a human spirit yields itself to its Almighty Lover, that moment He takes it, and assumes all responsibility, and makes Himself answerable for all its needs. There is but one condition: "Seek ye first the Kingdom of God, and His righteousness; and all these things shall be added unto you." As Queen Elizabeth said once to one of her Court: "Sir, if you will look after my business, I will make yours my care." Would that all the children of God might know what it is to hand over, moment by moment, as they occur, all worries, anxieties, and cares, to the compassionate Lord, sure that He takes them straight from their hands! We need never feel, then, as if all depended on our tired brain or failing strength, because the Lord Himself would supply all our need, according to his riches in glory. There is, indeed, no real independence for the believer. To be independent of Christ is to be cast forth as a branch to wither. The secret of rest, and fruit, and power, is an abiding union with Him—which time cannot impair, and death cannot dissolve.

Jacob was also in fear. What should hinder Esau, when he heard of his flight, from pursuing him? He was well acquainted with those parts;

was fleet of foot; or might use dogs, so as to track him and run him down. Besides, the country was full of robbers and wild beasts. And it was then that God calmed his fears, by showing him that that lone spot was teeming with angel-hosts, willing and eager to encamp about him, with celestial watch and ward. The most lonely spot is as safe for us as the most crowded, since God is there. It is His presence that keeps us safe amid the crowded city; and it is not in the smallest degree withdrawn when, benighted on some desolate moorland, we lay ourselves down to sleep. Into the low dungeon, where the true-hearted prophet lies (Lam. 3:55); into the prison cell, where the heroic apostle awaits his doom (Acts 23:11); into the cabin of the creaking, laboring vessel, threatened each moment with destruction (Acts 27:24)—there comes this assurance of One who cannot lie: "Fear not!" so that we may boldly say, "The Lord is my helper: and I will not fear what man shall do unto me" (Heb. 13:6).

II. THE ELEMENTS OF WHICH THIS REVELATION CONSISTED. The Spirit of God always conveyed His teachings to His servants in language borrowed from their surroundings. John's records of heaven are full of reminiscences of the Aegean; which sometimes murmured around the cliffs of his prison isle as a sea of glass bathed in fire, and at other times broke on them in yeasty foam. David's Psalms make constant reference to the wild hill country of Judea, in which so many of them were composed; Daniel's visions commemorate the giant forms familiar to him in Babylon; and Amos casts his prophecies in molds borrowed from a herdsman's life. So was it here.

Bethel was a bleak moorland that lay in the heart of Palestine. There was nothing remarkable about it; it was "a certain place." The hillsides and upland slopes were strewn with large sheets of bare rock: most of which lay flat upon their faces, like huge fallen gravestones; whilst some few were standing erect, like the cromlechs of our Druid circles.

Fleeing northwards, the wanderer suddenly found himself overtaken by the swift Eastern night, whilst on this desolate and unpeopled waste. There was no help for it but to lie down on the hard ground, taking the stones thereof as a pillow for his head. And thus he slept; and as he slept he dreamed: and in his dream his mind wove together many of his waking thoughts in fantastic medley. The striking appearance of those huge boulders; the memory that Abraham had built one of his earliest altars there, remnants of which may have been still standing; his last look upwards at that wondrous heaven, studded with the brilliant constellations of an Eastern night—all these wove themselves into his dreams. It seemed as if the huge slabs of limestone came near together, and built themselves up into a gigantic staircase, reaching from the spot where he lay to the starry depths above him; and on that staircase angels came and went, peopling by their multitudes that most desolate region, and evidently deeply concerned with the sleeper that lay beneath. Nor was this all; for, from the summit, the voice of God fell like music,

There are here three points of interest.

(1) *The Ladder.* Jacob may have been oppressed by a sense of his insignificance, and sin, and distance from home. And it was very pleasant to know that there was a link between him and God. Earth is not a wandering star: it is bound to heaven, not by the golden chains of which our Laureate sings; not by the iron fetters of necessity, as a slave ship to its captor; not by the silken ties of gravitation which thread the worlds—but by a ladder, denoting communion, fellowship, passage to and fro.

That ladder is Jesus Christ Himself (John 1:51). He took upon Himself our nature, built up from the dust; and in that nature passed upwards from the brow of Olivet, beyond principalities and powers, thrones and dominions, to the very throne of God: and in doing so, He has left a trail of light behind; and become "the way" by which we may approach the High and Lofty One that inhabits eternity, whose name is Holy. There is no other way; "no man cometh unto the Father but by Him." To neglect Him is to drift past the only medium by which a sinner may come into the Light and Love and Life of God. And yet the weakest and most sinful may climb through Jesus from the verge of the pit of hell to the foot of the eternal throne.

> The sons of Ignorance and Night
> May dwell in the Eternal Light
> Through the Eternal Love.

Milton, in his sublime poem, tells how Sin and Death followed the track of Satan, and paved after him a broad and beaten way over the dark abyss, whose boiling gulf tamely endured a bridge of wondrous length from hell, continued to the utmost orb of this frail world; so that the wicked spirits of his court might easily pass to and fro to tempt us mortals. *That* is imagination: *this* is fact, that there is a "Mediator between God and men, the Man Christ Jesus" (1 Tim. 2:5).

Sometimes, when the sky is beclouded, we do not see that across the garden path there sways a ladder of gossamer, linking tree with tree, but when the sun shines, it is revealed by its silver sheen. So, as the infidel looks upwards, he can see no bond of union between this atom of stardust and the metropolis of the universe, until his eyes are opened, and he sees the ladder left by the trail of the departing Savior. Thank God, we are not cut adrift to the mercy of every current; this dark coal ship is moored alongside the bright ship of heavenly grace; yes, and there is a plank from the one to the other.

(2) *The Angels.* The angels ascended: there is the ascent of our prayers. The angels descended: there is the descent of God's answers. We are reminded of the afferent and efferent nerves of the body—up which flash the sharp stings of pain from the extremities to the head; and down which come the directions how to act. It would be well to ponder more frequently the ministering care of the angels. They keep pace with every railway train, at whatever speed it travels, which bears some child of God to his appointed destination. They convoy every ship plowing its way through the troubled sea, which carries an heir of salvation to the haven where he would be. They encamp with horses and chariots of fire about every city, however beleaguered, in which God's servants are found. They minister to our needs. They prepare for us strengthening meals when we sink exhausted on the desert sands and wish to die. They whisper comfort into our troubled hearts. They carry our departing spirits upwards in the hour of death. "And all for love, and nothing for reward." God gives His angels charge concerning us, to keep us in *all* our ways; they bear us up in their hands. "The angel of the Lord encampeth round about them that fear Him, and delivereth them." They are "sent forth to minister to the heirs of salvation."

What comfort Jacob must have realized! He found, to his great surprise, that that lone spot was as thickly populated as *the gate* of some Eastern town, which is the place of concourse and barter. But it was *the gate of heaven;* for it seemed as if the populations of heaven were teeming around him, thronging to and fro; and all engaged in the beneficent work of bringing in the needs of men, and carrying out the blessings of God heaped up, after the overflowing measure with which He is wont to give. We need never yield to feelings of loneliness again, if we remember that, in our most retired hours, we are living in the very heart of a vast throng of angels; and we should hear their songs, and see their forms, if only our sense were not clogged with sin.

(3) *The Voice of God.* God answered his thoughts. He felt lonesome, but God said, "I will be with thee." He feared Esau, but God said, "I will keep thee." He knew not what hardships he might meet with; and God promised to bring him, safely back again. He seemed forsaken of friends, but God gave him the assurance, "I will not leave thee." Appearances seemed to contradict the Divine promise, but God said, "I will do that which I have spoken to thee of." These are precious words, but they only belong to those who lie at the foot of that wondrous Cross which unites earth with heaven. If your place is there, you may freely claim all the comfort that they contain.

Is it not remarkable that Jacob did not see these glorious realities until he slept? God was as much brooding in the wilderness before he slept as afterwards; *only he knew it not.* It was only when he slept that he came to know it. "Gradually slumber stole upon him, and folded him in her arms; gradually the fever cooled, the excitement subsided, the anxiety ceased. He grew tranquil and still; he lost himself—the flurried, heated, uneasy self that he had brought with him from Beersheba: and, *while he slept,* the hitherto unperceived Eternal Presence came out softly, largely, above and around him. He saw His glory, and heard His voice; the solitary waste trembled, flushed, and overflowed with God."*

It is impossible to walk with God, unless we have these seasons of quiet vision. Some are ever dwarfed, and driven to and fro by every

---

*Rev. S. A. Tipple.

wind, because they do not make times of respite from the whirl of occupation, and the fret of daily work and care. We need to escape from ourselves, our cares and gains, our personal individualities, in order that we may be at leisure to receive the revelations of God. And if we are to have this blessed sleep, it must be the gift of God in answer to our childlike trust.

In our next paper, we shall detail the effect which this marvelous vision produced on the awe-struck fugitive, but ere we close, we ask you to think of that mystic ladder, which descends from the throne of God to the spot, however lowly, where you may be, as you read these lines. It may be a moorland waste; a humble cottage; a ship's cabin; a settler's hut; a bed of pain: but Jesus Christ finds you out, and comes just where you are. The one pole of this ladder is the gold of His Deity; the other is the silver of His Manhood; the rungs are the series of events from the cradle of Bethlehem to the right hand of power, where He sits. That ladder sways beneath a weight of blessing for you. Oh that you would send away your burdens of sin and care and fear, by the hands of the ascending angels of prayer and faith, so as to be able to receive into your heart the trooping angels of peace, and joy, and love, and glory.

5

The Noble Resolve

Genesis 28

I slept and dreamt that life was beauty;
I waked and found that life was duty
Was thy dream, then, a shadowy lie?
Toil on, sad heart, courageously,
And thou shalt find thy dream to be
A noon-day light and truth to thee.
Dreams grow holy put in action,
Work grows fair through starry dreaming:
But where each flows on unmingling,
Both are fruitless and in vain.
A. A. Procter

We are studying the education of a human spirit in the story of Jacob, who became Israel the Prince. But before you can benefit by it, you must be quite sure that there is something in you capable of being educated. Education means *drawing out;* as culture will draw fragrance, color, and graceful beauty, out of the bulb which looks uninteresting and dead. No amount of education could draw such products from a stone. Education only avails when there is some latent germ containing the promise and potency of life. So the discipline of God will be a failure, so far as you are concerned, unless you have got within you, as Jacob certainly had, the principle of a nobler life than that which comes by nature. In a word—Have you been born again? Has there been placed within you, by the Spirit of God, the principle of a new and better life? Is there within you a something which is not of self, or of man, or of the will of the flesh, but of God? If so, you are welcome to acquire any help that may be afforded by a study of God's dealings with Jacob, in whose original constitution there was little to admire. There were *three steps* in God's dealings with this mean and crafty spirit; and, in one form or another, they have a universal application.

To begin with, God revealed Jacob to himself. He might have gone on for years in dreamy self-content, ignorant of the evils that lurked within his breast. So a strong temptation was permitted to cross his pathway. There was no necessity for him to yield, but he did yield. And in yielding, he stood face to face with the unutterable baseness of his own heart. A rock, jutting up in the midst of a stream, often reveals the set of the languid current. Fling a strong light into a cave: and the wretched tenants will hurry out screaming, as they behold the loathsome creatures that had crept around them. This is the first step towards soul health. A Nathan must be sent to unveil the evils that fester within, and to accost us with the terrible apostrophe. "Thou art the man!" If, of late, you have begun to see the hidden evils of your heart; and to discover the workings of things of which you could not have supposed yourself capable; and to loathe yourself, as Job did: then take heart. God is dealing with you; and is commencing a work which He will never abandon, till you are presented faultless in His presence, with exceeding joy. The first and indispensable work of the Holy Ghost, in the human spirit, is to convict of sin.

In the next place, God permitted Jacob to suffer the loss of all earthly friends and goods. The prodigal, in the far country, was reduced to heart rending straits. "When he had spent all, there arose a mighty famine in that land: and he began to be in want. And he was sent into the fields to feed swine; and no man gave unto him." And yet he was not much worse off than Jacob was at this moment. We saw in our last chapter that he was lonely, destitute, and in fear. He had little or no property, but a cruse of oil (v. 18) and his staff (32:10). He dreaded his brother's wrath. He was compelled to content himself with a stone for his pillow on the moorland waste. But he was not the last man who has had reason to bless God, to all eternity, for having swept his life clear of much which he had accounted absolutely needful to his existence. The "still small voice" can only be heard when all other voices are hushed. The silver stars can only be seen in the dark. It is when the weary fishers have toiled all the night, without taking a solitary fish, that they are prepared to see, in the morning haze, the form of One who loves them standing on the shore. Do not be surprised if to soul-trial there have been added other bitter trials beside.

Finally, God thrust in Jacob's life a revelation of His love. "Behold, a ladder set up on the earth, and the top of it reached to heaven." That ladder symbolized the love of God. All through his life, that love had surrounded Jacob with its balmy atmosphere, but he had never realized, or returned, or yielded to it. But now it was gathered up and crystallized into one definite appeal, and thrust upon him; so that he could do no other than behold it. And in that hour of conviction and need, it was as welcome as a ladder put down into a dark and noisome pit, where a man is sinking fast into despair; he quickly hails its seasonable aid, and begins to climb back to daylight.

Can you not remember the moment when the love of God in Jesus Christ first broke on you? You were deeply convinced of sin; you dreaded lest at any moment the sword of the Avenger should smite you down; you would have gladly exchanged places with the dumb animals around you; you were broken by trouble, anxiety, and care. And just then you were arrested by the cross of Jesus. At first you only looked on it with the casual gaze of curiosity, but as you looked, your attention became so fixed that you were spellbound. You saw it transfigured beneath the light of heaven; you felt that Divine love shone in those dying eyes; and streamed in tides of blessing from every open wound; and spoke in every accent of that faltering voice. And as you lingered still, there stole into your heart the conviction that it was all for you—a conviction which forced tears to your eyes, and these words from your lips: "He loved *me,* and gave Himself for *me. My* sins nailed Him there; *my* curse poured its vials upon that drooping head; *my* stripes broke that royal heart."

"So I saw in my dream, that just as Christian came up with the cross, his burden loosed from off his shoulders, and fell from off his back, and began to tremble; and so continued to do till it came to the mouth of the sepulcher, where it fell in, and I saw it no more. Then was Christian glad and lightsome; and said, with a merry heart,

> He hath given me rest by His sorrow,
> And life by His death.

Then he stood still awhile to look and wonder; even till the springs that were in his head sent the waters down his cheeks."

Has this been your experience? If not, seek it; ask that your eyes may be opened to see the love of God to you, revealed in the cross of Jesus, and let down into your life. Then will you also give three leaps for joy, and go on your way singing.

The revelation of God's love will have five results on the receptive spirit.

I. IT WILL MAKE US QUICK TO DISCOVER GOD. Jacob had been inclined to localize God in his father's tents: as many localize Him now in chapel, church, or minister; supposing that prayer and worship are more acceptable there than anywhere beside. *Now* he learned that God was equally in every place—on the moorland waste as well as by Isaac's altar, though his eye had been too blind to perceive Him. In point of fact, the difference lay not in God, but in *himself,* the human spirit carries with it everywhere its own atmosphere, through which it may see, or not see, the presence of the Omnipresent. If your spirit is reverent, it will discern God on a moorland waste. If your spirit is thoughtless and careless, it will fail to find Him even in the face of Jesus Christ. There are many men, who might have kept as close to the Apostle Paul as his shadow, who would not have seen one angel vision or heard one heavenly word. On the other hand, if the Apostle were to spend a day with us, he would see traces of the glorious presence of God in our busy streets and wrangling marts. The difference is not in the place, or in the degrees of God's presence, but in the keenness of the spiritual eye, since all places are equally hallowed, and God is everywhere.

When we have been touched and solemnized by some stately service or stirring discourse, we are disposed to say, "This is none other but the house of God; and this is the gate of heaven." But we are not disposed to say as much of the shop or counting house in which we spend the greater part of our time. The reason for this is to be found in the materialism of our spirit. If only we were full of God, we should find that every spot was sacred, every moment hallowed, every act a sacrament; from every incident we should see a ladder stretching up to heaven: and our happy spirits would be constantly availing themselves of the opportunity to run up the shining way and embrace their dearest Lord.

Similarly, when we have met with a great deliverance—as Abraham on Mount Moriah—we are led to exclaim, "This is the finger of God." But we are not apt to say as much of every trivial incident in daily life. The reason, again, is in ourselves. We need the quick insight which only love can give. It was the disciple to whom Jesus had revealed His special love that discerned Him on the lakeshore, and cried, "It is the Lord." And if we were as willing as he was to drink in the love of Jesus, we should be as quick as he was in discerning the presence of the Lord.

Up to this moment, the Lord has been in many of the moorland wastes of your lives, but *you have not known it.* He has been beside you in that lonely chamber of pain; in that irksome situation; on that rugged pathway; by that bitter cross; amid those godless companions; during those hours which you have counted secular and profane—but your eyes have been holden. What wonder that your path has been so drear! But if you will only take home to yourself the message of the cross of Jesus, "God loves me"; and if you will let it shed its perfume through your secret heart—then you will never feel lonely or outcast again. You will be able to see Him where no other eye can discern Him. You will feel the ruddy glow of His love when others carry chilled and torpid hearts. You will discover that a desolate moor is one of the mansions of your Father's house. You will detect your Father's hand-writing in every letter; your Father's seal on every parcel; your Father's will in every event. You will be able to commune with Him equally on the hillside as amid the congregation. And you will be often compelled to exclaim, as you meet with fresh revelations of Himself, in the most unlikely places, *"This* is none other but the house of God; and *this* is the gate of heaven."

II. It Will Inspire Us With Godly Fear. "He was afraid, and said, How dreadful is this place!" "Perfect love casteth out fear"—the fear that hath torment, but it begets us in another fear, which is the beginning of wisdom and the foundation of all noble lives; the fear that reveres God, and shudders to grieve Him; and dreads to lose the tiniest chance of doing His holy will. True love is always fearless and fearful. It is fearless with the freedom of undoubting trust, but it is fearful lest it should miss a single grain of tender affection, or should bring a moment's shadow over the face of the beloved. Those who look from without sometimes rebuke us for dwelling so constantly on the infinite love of God, surrounding us, as the warm Southern seas lap around shores enameled with shells. Some say, "You will lead people to live loosely, if you tell them that there is no sin which may not be instantly forgiven." Ah! they do not know that there are none who fear sin so much as those who know that they are greatly loved. For them every spot is full of the presence of the Beloved. Heaven itself does not more evidently glow with it than each spot of earth. And thus, though all other fear has fled before all-mastering love, there will have come into the spirit another fear, which distrusts self and clings to Christ, and works out its salvation with fear and trembling.

III. IT WILL CONSTRAIN US TO GIVE OURSELVES TO GOD. The ordinary reading might lead us to suppose that, true to his worse self, Jacob tried to make a bargain with God; and promised to take Him as his, on certain conditions. "*If* God will be with me, and keep me in my way, and give me bread to eat and raiment to put on: *then*—" But a better reading relieves him of this sad imputation; and tones the words down to mean that if the Lord would be his God, then the stone should be God's house. But, however the words may run, this was evidently the moment of his consecration. He was constrained by love of God, "no longer to live to himself, but to Him."

Have you done thus, dear reader? It is the sole condition of soul health, and peace, and power. You are Christ's by right, but you have been living as if you were your own, and had never been bought by His precious blood. Is it then to be wondered at, that your life has been such a miserable failure? You are robbing Jesus of His own purchased possession; and you cannot expect to enjoy the fullness of His salvation. Give yourself to Him now. And, as soon as you will to do so, He takes that which you give. Or, if you cannot give yourself, then lie low at His feet, and ask Him to take all you are and have. And so soon as the words have passed your lips, He will answer your prayer, and make you His forever.

IV. It Will Prompt Us to Devote our Property to Him. "Of all that Thou shalt give me, I will surely give the tenth unto Thee." There is no reason to doubt that this became the principle of Jacob's life: and if so, he shames the majority of Christian people—most of whom do not give on principle; and give a very uncertain and meager percentage of their income. The Church would have no lack if every one of its members acted upon this principle. Let the proportion be diminished, if you will; though *that* were surely unworthy of us, who sing,

> Were the whole realm of nature mine,
> That were an offering far too small;
> Love so amazing, so divine,
> Demands my life, my soul, my all.

But whether the proportion be diminished or not, let each Christian person resolve to give systematically to the Lord's cause; and to put aside, as firstfruits from all profits and receipts, a certain part, which shall be considered as distinctly and exclusively the Lord's, to be applied as He may direct.

There is something better than this—viz., to consider oneself, one's earnings, one's strength, one's all, as belonging to the dear Master; as the rages, and earnings, and jewels, of slaves belonged absolutely to their owners, who had bought them off the block. But many, admitting this theoretically, do nothing practically; and, therefore, it is better to give a regular proportion certainly, and as much more as you choose, as a perpetual reminder that all you have and are is not your own, but Jesus Christ's.

It is failure in this which so often brings barrenness and joylessness into Christian lives. This is the reason that so many of the ascending angels never come down again, or return with empty hands. This is why we sow much, and bring in little; eat, and have not enough; drink, and are not satisfied; and put our wages into a bag with holes. We have robbed God in tithes and offerings. But if we would resolve to give Him tithes of all, and to bring them into His storehouse, we should find that He would open the windows of heaven, and pour us out such a blessing that there would not be room to receive it.

V. IT WILL FILL US WITH JOY. "Then Jacob lifted up his feet" (29:1, *marg.*). Does not that denote the lighthearted alacrity with which he sped upon his way? His feet were winged with joy, and seemed scarcely to tread the earth. All sorrow had gone from his heart; for he had handed his burdens over to those ascending angels. And this will be our happy lot, if only we will believe the love that God hath to us. We, too, shall lose our burdens at the foot of the cross; and we shall learn the blessed secret of handing over, as soon as they arise, all worries and fears to our pitiful High Priest. Then shall our mouth be "filled with laughter, and our tongue with singing." Our heart shall "bubble over with good matter." "Our soul shall make her boast in the Lord; the humble shall hear thereof, and be glad."

❧ 6

The Education of Home

Life is only bright when it proceedeth
Towards a truer, deeper Life above;
Human Love is sweetest when it leadeth
To a more Divine and perfect Love.
A. A. Procter

Genesis 29

Next to the love of God comes the love of man or woman, as a factor in the education of a human spirit. Each one of us is capable of giving out a vast wealth of love; we must love and be loved: and almost everything depends on the twin spirit whom we choose as the object of our affection; and as the hearth at whose fires we may warm ourselves, when chilled and repelled by an unfriendly world. That love may make or mar us; may transfigure or degrade us—and which it shall be is settled by the objects whom we choose, and the way in which we treat them.

Jacob's encounter with Rachel at the first well he came to reminds us that though there is nothing more important than the union of heart with heart, there is nothing into which people drift more heedlessly. A fancy, a look, a smile, a touch, a moment's talk in a crowded room, amid the excitement of an evening's gaiety—any of these is deemed sufficient to justify a choice which may affect the destiny of the spirit forever.

Of course we do not deny that Jacob may find his other self in the beautiful girl at the well, under the Eastern noon; and that she may prove to be the one without whom his life would be incomplete. It may so happen, through the kind providence of God, which shields us from dangers we do not perceive, and loads us with benefits we do not deserve. Nevertheless, it is the highest folly to leave so momentous a matter to be decided by a transient passion, or by the charms of a fascinating manner and pretty face. Do not carry your heart on your sleeve. Do not let your affections trail loosely on the ground, to catch in every thorn-brake. Gird up the loins of your mind; test the spirits whether they be of God. Do not take an irrevocable step without earnest prayer that He will still the voices of self-choice; keep you from making a mistake; and reveal to you His will.

It is not enough to think and pray thus when a new affection has already flung its spell over you. At such a time, the soul is thrilling beneath its new-found rapture; and it is much harder for the judgment to discover the voice of God, because the heart deflects it—as the mass of iron in a modern steamboat deflects the needle from the pole. And therefore, it is of the highest importance that these subjects be made a matter of prayer and thought in the earlier stages of life, when a supreme affection is, as yet, an ideal and a dream. Let mothers speak of them to their daughters; and fathers to their sons—as Isaac did to Jacob (28:1, 2). Let young men, whenever they think of these matters, turn their thoughts into prayers that God would guide them—as He did Abraham's servant—to the woman whom He has chosen to be their helpmeet. And let Christian women lay aside all ideas of attracting men to themselves. Let them quiet their hearts as weaned babes. Let them constitute themselves the wards of God: leaving Him to choose for them the one who shall give them strength for sweetness; defense for weakness; protection for helplessness; and love for love.

There is no training of such value to man or woman as the training of the home—to which the deep instincts of our nature, and the most solemn sanctions of the Bible, point us. Jacob found it so. Rachel and Leah had a very powerful influence upon his character and life; and we need to take warning by his mistakes, and reap his rewards.

I. THE FOUR CONDITIONS OF A TRUE HOME. (1) *There must be a supreme affection.* This was clearly a love match. "Jacob loved Rachel" (v. 18), is a sufficient explanation. And no marriage is heaven made, heaven sent, or heaven sanctioned, which does not spring from a supreme love. Alas, how many marry from some less worthy motive! Some for a home; others to escape from uncongenial surroundings; others for position; others for baser reasons still. All these sin against God's purpose; they sin against one another; and, not least, they sin against themselves. No two should marry unless each feels that life without the other would be incomplete. Less than this will never suffice. If one loves, and not the other, there cannot be true happiness for there is no reciprocity; no mutual satisfaction. To give without receiving is to run to waste; to take without giving is to harden the heart, till it becomes ice. If neither loves, what is it less than the crime which cries myriad-tongued to heaven on every night breeze? But if there be true love, then, though one has been taken from the other by death before they stand together at the marriage altar, yet in the sight of God's high angels those twain are one forever.

It is needless to show how the necessity of the presence of a supreme love is the ground and justification of monogamy, the union of two. This has been the pride and glory of the German peoples, as even Tacitus discerned; and this has been the cradle of all those higher ministries which distinguish our people, and assign us the leading position among the nations of the earth. "Therefore take heed to your spirit, and let none deal treacherously against the wife of his youth."

You have no right to excite that love, or play with it, unless you are prepared to satisfy it, as far as you may. You have no right to give that love away, till you discover that all other conditions are assured. You have no right to marry if this love be absent. You would have no right to treat either man or woman as you would not like your brother or sister to be treated, or as you would not like to be treated yourself.

(2) *Marriage must be "only in the Lord."* Jacob's was so. He might have taken a wife of the daughters of Heth, as Esau did, steeped in the idolatries and impurities which cursed the land. But, guided by his parents' counsels, he crossed the desert to obtain a wife who had been reared in a home in which there lingered still the memory of the worship of the God of Abraham, of Nahor, and of their father Terah (31:53).

The Bible rings from end to end with warnings against mixed marriages. "Thou shalt not give thy daughter unto his son; nor take his

daughter unto thy son; for they will turn away thy son from following
Me, to serve other gods" (Deut. 7:3). "Be ye not unequally yoked together with unbelievers; for what fellowship hath righteousness with
unrighteousness; light with darkness; Christ with Belial?" (2 Cor. 7:14,
15). "She is at liberty to be married to whom she will; only in the
Lord?" (2 Cor. 7:39).

We need not be surprised at these strong and repeated prohibi-
tions. A mixed marriage is a prolific source of misery. In the course of
a considerable pastoral experience, I have never known one to result in
perfect happiness. Believers, in such unions, do not level their unbe-
lieving partners up to Christ, but are themselves dragged down to infinite misery and self-reproach. "Did not Solomon, king of Israel, sin
by these things? Yet among many nations was there no king like unto
him, who was beloved of his God: and God made him king over all
Israel. Nevertheless, even him did outlandish women cause to sin"
(Neh. 13:26). How can there be sympathy in the deepest matters? Each
feels that there is one subject on which they are not agreed; and this is
a fatal barrier to perfect union. The ungodly partner despises the
Christian for marrying in the teeth of principle. The Christian is disappointed because the apparent influence gained before marriage is
dissipated soon after the knot is irrevocably tied. Well might Rebekah
be weary of her life through those daughters of Heth! Many a Christian
girl has married an unbeliever, in the hope of saving him, and has bitterly rued her choice: she has seen her influence wane; and has learned,
though too late, that the Holy Spirit will not cooperate with our efforts,
if they are based on distinct disobedience to one of the clearest commands of the Bible. If a man threatens that if you deny yourself to him,
he will take violent or fatal steps, *let him!* He has no right to put you
in that position; he simply wants to get you into his power: and he will
be much too great a coward to carry out his threats. Do right in the
sight of God; and leave *him* to settle the matter with his Maker.

(3) *A true home should be based on the goodwill of parents and friends.*
This is not necessary where sanction is withheld from caprice. But
where it can possibly be obtained, there is the halo of a brighter promise encircling the union of two young hearts, when it is ratified amid
the congratulations of rejoicing friends. So it was with Jacob: "Isaac

called Jacob, and blessed him, and sent him away" (Gen. 28:1–5). It is wise and right, where practicable, for children to consult, in such matters, those whose love has made them the eager guardians of their opening life; and to do so by courtesy, even when mature years have given them the right to choose and act for themselves. But if parents would have such confidences when their children are old, they must make themselves their confidants while they are young; they must give as well as receive; they must exercise their authority by love and reasoning, rather than by constraint; and they have no right to let their decision be warped, through any personal whim, from the straight line of what would best serve the highest interest of a beloved child.

(4) *There should be some prospect of suitable livelihood.* In the broad wealthy land where Jacob found himself, there was not much difficult about that. It is a much more complicated matter amid the conditions of our crowded modern life. Yet there ought to be some security of a competence. Young people have no need to begin where their parents are leaving off; to do so would avoid much wholesome difficulty and the opportunities for mutual help: but it is equally absurd to run the risk of a late repentance for a rash marriage. Young man, select as your partner one who, with refinement and culture, is not above turning her hands to the practical details of household management, and who knows what to do and how to do it. Young women, give your hearts to men who love you well enough to earn you through years of faithful and steadfast courtship, if so it must be. Anyone could do one deed of gallantry; it took a true man to serve for seven long years.

If these four conditions are fulfilled, there will be the strongest reasons for anticipating a union which shall be a miniature picture of that sublime event for which the whole creation groans: when the midnight air shall be startled by the tidings of the Bridegroom's advent; and the Church shall pass as the Bride into the wedding feast.

II. THE EXPULSIVE POWER OF SUPREME AFFECTION. "Jacob served seven years for Rachel; and they seemed unto him but a few days, for the love he had to her" (v. 20). That sentence always charms us for its beauty and its truth. Love has the power of making a rough road easy, and a weary waiting time short. It makes us oblivious to many things, which, for lack of it, would be insupportable. The three mighty men break through the armed host of the Philistines, to get one draft of water from the well for their beloved chieftain, oblivious of personal risk—*the love they bare to him.* The trembling women, on the resurrection morning, ventured out into the perils of the crowded city, while it was yet dark, that they might embalm the body of their Lord; nor do they appear to have considered the perils amid which they threaded their way to His grave—*for the love they bare to Him.* The martyrs died amid bitter torture, with a smile on their faces and a song on their lips, not counting their lives dear, but reckoning it an honor to spill their heart's blood—*for the love they bare to Him.* Many a woman has nursed her children through loathsome disorders, doing for them what no money would hire a servant to do, but she has not considered the cost—*for the love she bare to them.* Yea, Jesus Christ Himself endured the cross, and despised the shame; stooped to a felon's death; bore the base treatment of coarse and brutal soldiery; and rejoiced to lay down His life—*for the love He bare to us.*

Do you find it hard to deny yourself, to make the required sacrifices for doing His will, and to confess Him? There is one cure, a short and easy one. Go to the Holy Ghost, and ask Him to shed the love of Christ abroad in your heart, and so teach you to love Him who first loved you. Then, as the tides of that love rise within your heart, they will constrain you to live, not for yourself, but for Him; then burdens will be light that once crushed; roads will be pleasant that once strained and tired; hours will fly that were once leaden-footed; years will seem as a day. Love's labor is always light.

III. Some Closing Words. Are you unmarried? Do not bewail yourself, as if your life must be incomplete. Yours is not a higher state, as the priest has falsely taught, but it is neither a failure nor a shame. It will attain to finished beauty, if only you walk in the path which your Heavenly Father has prepared for you. Cease to measure yourself by human standards. Find rest in being just what your Heavenly Father wills you to be. Break the alabaster box of your affection on Him, and His, for His sake. It may be that you have been kept free from the limited circle of a home, in order to pour your love on those who have no one else to love them. But remember, it is possible for all such to live in perfect self-restraint and purity, through the power of the Holy Ghost, "which is in us."

Are you disappointed? Jacob was disappointed in poor Leah; and she spent many a bitter hour of anguish. Her father had forced her on a man who did not love her, and who wanted to be rid of her. She had a woman's heart, and pined for love that never came. There are few stories more touching than the secret history of Leah, as revealed in the names she gave her boys, and her reasons in giving them. Yet remember, she had her compensations in the love of those strong, healthy lads, who greeted her with the title, "Mother," so dear to a woman's heart. And there are, doubtless, compensations in your lot, if you are not too bitter to see them. And this is the best of all: "The Lord will look upon your affliction" (v. 32). Meanwhile, do not flinch from doing your duty as in His sight.

Are you happily married? Then beware lest you make an idol of your happiness; or suppose that there is no further need to watch. Is it not remarkable that Jacob's dearest wife was the source of his defeat and disgrace, in after years, because he hid in her baggage the household idols of her father? That was a remarkable command that Moses gave to Israel: "If the wife of thy bosom entice thee secretly, saying, Let us go and serve other gods, thou shalt not consent unto her; neither shalt thou spare, but thine hand shalt be first upon her to put her to death." Does it not teach us that we are not to receive, without question, the suggestions of even our dearest? We must ever put God first. "If any come to Me, and hate not his father, and mother, and wife, and children, and brethren, and sisters, yea, and his own life also, he cannot be My disciple."

Have you become a Christian since you were married to an unbeliever? Then do not seek, in any wise, to alter your relations (1 Cor. 7:13, 14), but expect, in all assurance, that you will be the happy means of winning that beloved one to Christ. And seek this, not so much by frequent speech—there is a time to speak, but also a time to be silent—but rather seek it by the admirable beauty and consistency of your life: "That if any obey not the word, they may without the word be gained by your manner of life beholding your behavior" (1 Pet. 3:1).

Above all, withhold not your love from the dear Master, Christ. Hold all human love in Him. You may love to the uttermost of your power, if only you make Him first; and take your love as His gift; and enjoy it in Him; and thank Him for it. So human love will teach you to understand Divine love; and from your thoughts you may understand His thoughts: "Every one that loveth . . . knoweth God." "That being rooted and grounded in love, we may be able to comprehend . . . the love of Christ."

❦ 7

The Mid-Passage of Life

Let us, then, be what we are:
And speak what we think;
And in all things keep ourselves loyal to truth
And the sacred professions of friendship.
Of all that is unsound, beware!
Longfellow

Genesis 30

In our last chapter, we saw how Jacob built for himself a home. But ah—what a home! The presence of the two sisters there was fatal to its peace. They who had been happy enough as sisters before he came, could not now live in such close quarters, as wives of the same husband, without incessant jealousy and heart-burning. Each had her own grievance. Poor Leah knew that Jacob had never loved her; and that she was not the wife of his choice: and though God compensated her by giving her that pride of Oriental women, a family of sons, yet even this was a new source of anguish to her; for Rachel envied her. Frightfully desolate was she in that home; and the names of her sons are like so many landmarks of her misery. But Rachel must have been equally miserable: true, she had her husband's love, but she could not be sure of keeping it; and she had the mortification of seeing her sister's children growing up as her husband's heirs. How eagerly she prayed, and fretted, proudly chafed!

What wonder, then, that the children grew up wild and bad? Reuben, unstable as water, excitable and passionate; Simeon, quick to obey, but quick to desperate cruelty; and Levi, a willing accomplice in his crime. When children turn out badly, and the beautiful fate of childhood does not lead to the fair temple of mature life, it is generally the fault of the home training; and it is more often the result of what they see than of what they are taught. Whatever Jacob may have been—and I fear that his example was none of the best—yet the impressions received in the women's tents, of high words and evil passion, would be enough to ruin any child. Beware how you act at home. Remember what keen little eyes are watching you; and with what absolute mimicry they will repeat what they see.

But it is not so much Jacob's home life, as his business dealings, that we have now to consider.

He served fourteen years, as a dowry for his two wives; and at the time when Rachel gave birth to her firstborn Joseph, that period had elapsed. So soon as mother and child were able to undertake so long and fatiguing a journey, Jacob declared his intention of returning to Canaan; and this resolve was perhaps precipitated by a message from Rebekah, to say that there was now no further reason for his absence.

This proposal alarmed Laban, who had learned to value his services; and was much too astute to let him go, without making an effort to retain so valuable a servant. "Tarry," said he, "I pray thee, if I have found favor in thine eyes; for I have learned by experience that the Lord hath blessed me for thy sake." Jacob at once caught at the opportunity of making an independent provision for his large and increasing family; and the bargain was struck.

Eastern sheep are almost wholly white; the goats black; the particolored rare. Jacob proposed, therefore, that all the brown and speckled should be at once removed; and that all of that color, which the flock produced afterwards should be his wage. There was no harm in this; unless he had already made up his mind to take the unfair advantage of Laban, which is a dark blot on his name. Supposing that this were the case, we have here a humiliating picture of two unprincipled men, each trying to outwit the other: Laban chuckling over his bargain, and taking care to remove, not only the young, but the old, and sending them off under the care of his sons; Jacob, laughing in his sleeve, because he knew, or thought he knew, a plan of winning to himself a great advantage. But whether this were premeditated in the first instance or not, it is certain that Jacob acted as a cheat and a rogue. Laban entrusted his flocks to his care without supposing for a moment that he would tamper with the usual course of nature. Jacob, on the other hand, did not scruple to use every art to secure his own advantage at Laban's cost; taking means to procure for himself the produce of the strongest of the flock, and to leave to Laban the enfeebled and the weak.

It is very surprising to find how eagerly some of the older commentators try to vindicate Jacob in this. They might almost as soon sprinkle rosewater on a sewer. And it certainly lowers the standard of morality to attempt to prove that there was not very much harm after all in what Jacob did. I feel no temptation to do this.

The Bible does not hesitate to tell us the very worst about its heroes; that we may better magnify the grace of God, which, out of such materials, could create trophies of mercy. Let Jacob be painted in colors borrowed from Rembrandt's brush; and there is all the more wonder that the grace of God could overcome his duplicity and cunning, and make of him a diamond of the very first water.

Let us draw near, and remonstrate with Jacob, as he sits beside his flocks, in the scorching Eastern sun; and let us carefully notice his excuses and pleas.

He might urge, first, the necessity of self-protection. "My uncle is bent on defrauding me, and keeping me down; and, if I did not do this, he would succeed. You must meet a man on his own ground; and, as he has chosen to play the rogue with me, I cannot see the harm of turning his own weapons on himself." This reasoning did not die with Jacob: it is still passed round the world in act and word; and good men are sometimes sorely tempted to make use of it. It is undoubtedly hard to find that another man is taking an unfair advantage of you by maneuvers which, from your soul, you loathe. But is that a justification for you to resort to them? This has come into your life as a test; to prove whether you believe the world is ordered by God or the devil. If you believe it is the devil's world, it is quite likely that you will try to hold your ground, or gain an advantage by arts, which he alone would approve. But if you really believe in the Almighty God, you will be sure that falsehood must ultimately fail, and righteousness finally win: and you will meet fraud by faith; cunning by conscience; and violence by a Divine virtue. Goliath may wear armor, but that is no reason why David should. Remember how the Lord hath said: "I will keep thee." Your competitors may do mean and dirty tricks, but you will live to see them trapped in their own pits, and pierced by their own swords: while if you continue to do right, you will go steadily forward to success; as the sun at noon rids himself of the clouds that obscured his early rays. "Trust in the Lord, and do good; so shalt thou dwell in the land, verily thou shalt be fed. Fret not thyself in any wise to do evil; for evildoers shall be cut off." "The Lord shall be thy confidence, and shall keep thy foot from being taken."

He might urge, as a second plea, the familiar formula. Business is business. "It is quite right to speak of Bethel when that scared anniversary comes round, but it is out of the question to suppose that I can act and speak in my daily business, as I did when that angel ladder glistened before my view. Business must be regulated on its own distinct laws; and they are quite different to those which obtain at Bethel." It is strange to hear professing Christians speak thus. They have one standard of morality for the Lord's day; and another for the other six. They permit things in business which are contrary to the spirit and letter of the Word of God; and which they would not sanction for a moment in the ordinary dealings of daily life; and they quiet their conscience by the easy motto, Business is business. I never can understand what difference there is in the morality of an act, because it has to do with buying and selling; or why we should not apply to such an act the same principles by which we judge other actions. According to the practice of some, we should read the golden rule thus: "Do as you would be done by—except in business." "Do not steal" applies everywhere—except in shops and factories. "Lying lips are always an abomination to the Lord"—except when a salesman wants to dispose of some soiled goods. If this were the case, the larger part of the life of most men would be outside the circumference of God's commands. But it cannot be. The moralities of the Gospel resemble the law of gravitation: to which nothing is secular; nothing common, but which determines the pathway of a grain of dust on the autumn breeze, as well as the march of worlds.

But Jacob might urge, as his third plea, that this was the general practice. "Other shepherds practice it. Laban must know all about it; or he might know. When you are with Chaldeans, you must do as Chaldeans do. I am not worse than others." But a universal practice does not condone sin; this is the difference between God's laws and man's. Let all men break a human law: it stands abrogated on the statute book; it cannot be enforced. But though all men break a Divine law, it will exact its penalty from all. Multitudes may have sinned together, but they will not be able to screen each other, or to escape. And if you do a mean thing, it will come back to roost in you heart; and will find you out with its curse, though you may be one of a crowd.

But he might urge, as his fourth plea, that chicanery was necessary to obtain bread. "A man must live, you know." But the plea cannot stand. There is no *must* about it. Where should we have been today if all the martyrs had argued that it was more important to live than to do right? Every man has to choose between these two. Many men deem life more important than righteousness; and, like the nautilus, they drop out of sight when storms sweep the sea: they are fair weather Christians, and are of too soft a stuff to make martyrs. Others reckoned that it is not necessary for them to live, but it is necessary for them to do right. They say what Pompey said when his friends besought him not to risk his life upon a tempestuous sea—"It is necessary for me to go; it is not necessary for me to live." This surely is the logic of faith. A man may be well content to suffer the loss of all things, and to die, if he may keep inviolate the priceless jewels which God has entrusted to his care.

Jacob's double-dealing appeared to be a success. "The man increased exceedingly; and had much cattle, and maidservants, and menservants, and camels, and asses." But that which men call success, and which is sometimes a very superficial and temporary thing, proves nothing as to the rightness or wrongness of a life. It is not by the glitter of gold that God rewards His faithful servants. Many a noble life in the sight of God has been a sad failure, when judged by human standards. And many a failure in the judgment of man has been a royal success in the estimation of the angels. When a tide of gold has been setting in towards some men, it has been allowed to come as a judgment and a curse, that they might be blinded to destruction. And in many cases, the tide has been restrained, that it might be more possible for the soul to attain to perfect health.

I demur to the common use of the phrase, "Honesty is the best policy"; no doubt, it is so in reality and at the end, though not always in appearance and at the beginning. But if we are simply going to be honest because it pays, we are basing the fabric of our lives on too low a level; and our foundation may give way in days of storm. We must be honest—not because of good policy, but because of good principle, because it is right, and noble, and God-like; yea, because it pleases God. Let us do right; and we shall be happier with scanty means and a good conscience, than those who have all that a heart could wish, but are haunted by memories of the means by which their fortunes were acquired—memories which, like the ghost of the murdered king, in the immortal drama, arise to mar the merriment of the splendid feast. "A little that a righteous man hath is better than the riches of many wicked."

Do not draw a line of separation between the house of God and the house of business. The counting house and the shop may be as much the house of God as the holiest shrine, where generations have knelt in prayer. A devout soul will find God everywhere; and will abide with God in every calling in which it is called. If you cannot have the companionship of Jesus in the paths of daily business, by all means abandon them. But if they are at all legitimate, you will find Him at your side, though His presence is veiled from all other eyes.

Do what you have to do in the name of the Lord Jesus. In that name you are wont to pray. In that name learn to do your work. Speak that name over the most menial tasks; and they will glisten with heavenly beauty. Speak it over doubtful things; and their true character will be revealed—as the tempter sprang from the toad, when touched by the spear of Ithuriel. Speak it over difficulties; and the iron gates will own the spell, and open to you of their own accord.

Take the Lord Jesus into your partnership. Consult Him before branching out into new directions; or consigning goods to fresh customers; or making large purchases. Let every transaction and every entry be freely open to His eye. Let every transaction be laid before

Him, for Him to close or open as He will. And be sure to divide with Him the profits, which are His due. A business life, with such sanctions, could never strand on the shoals of bankruptcy.

Above all, realize that you are the *slaves* of Jesus Christ. In the olden days of slavery, a master would sometimes put a trusted slave into a position of great responsibility, where he was permitted even to trade for his owner. But his brains, his muscles, and his gains were all another's. Everything had to be used and accounted for on that one condition. And what are we but the purchased possession of the Son of God? What is our business, but a branch of our stewardship for Him, as it is also a training school for us? What is there we can call our own? It is He that gives us power to get wealth; and His image and superscription are evident on every coin. "Ye are not your own; ye are bought with a price: wherefore glorify God in your body and in your spirit, which are God's."

8

The Stirring Up
of the Nest

O Father! the untrodden path how shall we dare to tread?
We see not what is in the clouds now hanging o'er our head.
Thou hid'st the future from our ken. Oh, be Thy children's light!
Guide Thou our halting footsteps in the day or in the night.
Marianne Farningham

Genesis 31

I
n that sublime song with which the great Lawgiver closed his words
to Israel, we are carried through the steeps of air, to stand beside an
eagle's eyrie, perched amid the inaccessible cliffs. Here we may find
a clue to explain the ways of God to man. The young eaglets are old and
strong enough to fly, but they cling to the familiar nest, with its scant
shelter. They dare not venture forth upon the untried air, or trust their
fluttering wings. But they *must* learn to fly. There are joys awaiting
them in the wide oceans of space, which far outvie those of the rude
nest in which they have been nurtured. And so the eagle stirs up the
nest, and drives them forth. What anguish the young birds feel, as they
see that nest destroyed; and themselves thrust forth, as it might seem,
to certain destruction! But when once they are launched upon the up-
bearing air, and learn by glad experience the freedom, the ecstasy of
flight—how grateful should they be to the parent bird, who flinched
not from the unwelcome task; and who still swoops and flies beneath
them, ready to catch them up if their powers should flag, and to bear
them sunwards. There, in mid-heaven, she lets them fall again; and
again she catches them: and thus, each moment they increase in

confidence and strength; and develop powers of sustained flight, of which they were unconscious when they lingered by the nest.

It is a beautiful parable of human life. We all cling to the old nest—the old home where we were born; the dear protection of strong, true hearts, that screen us from every breath; the place where we are known; the faces with which we are familiar; the competence which we have won. We say, with eager petulance, "Let us stay here forever. Do not speak to us of that great outer world; or of the opportunities which lie hidden there; and which, you say, might bring out powers of muscle, and brain, and heart, of which we now know nothing. We would rather that they should remain hidden, than that we should have to suffer the anguish of their development amid the strain and trial of that rude, strange world of which we now catch but distant rumors. We are content; let us stay." But the great love of God has provided some better thing for us. He knows that there are heights and depths of life hidden from us till we go forth. Keen may be the agony of the moment in which we see the nest stirred up, and find ourselves flung forth into a strange element. But it is not worthy to be compared with the glory instantly revealed; for that light affliction, which is but for a moment, works out for us a far more exceeding and eternal weight of glory: the glory of a faith that poises itself on the unseen; the glory of a hope that breasts the thundercloud; the glory of a love that soars ever upward to the sun. "They change their strength, and mount up with wings as eagles."

These thoughts give the key to the next experience in Jacob's troubled life. There is reason for every step in our education, whether we see it or not: and, though Jacob could not have guessed it at the time, yet, as we look back, we can easily understand why his residence at Haran was suddenly closed; and his home broken up; and he driven across the desert, as a fugitive, hotly pursued—much as he had been years before, only in the reverse direction.

In point of fact, Jacob was becoming too contented in that strange land. Like Ulysses and his crews, he was in danger of forgetting the land of his birth; the tents of his father; and the promises of which he was the heir. He was fast losing the pilgrim spirit, and settled into a citizen of that far country. His mean and crafty arts to increase his wealth were honeycombing his spirit, and eating out his nobler nature, prostituting it to the meanest ends. His wives, infected with the idolatry of their father's house, were in danger of corrupting the minds of his children; and how then would fare the holy seed, destined to give the world the messages of God? It was evident that his nest must be broken up in Haran; that he must be driven back into the pilgrim life— to become a stranger and a sojourner, as his fathers were. And this was another step nearer the moment when he became an Israel, a prince with God. This may be your destiny, my reader; and, if it be, accept meekly the discipline which forces you towards it. It is the hand that was pierced with nails that breaks up the nest of the past, and beckons you to the untried but blessed realities in front.

I. THE SUMMONS TO DEPART. "And the Lord said unto Jacob, Return unto the land of thy fathers, and to thy kindred; and I will be with thee." Whether there was voice audible to the outward ear I cannot tell, but there was certainly the uprising of a strong impulse within his heart. Sometimes on a sultry summer day we suddenly feel the breeze fanning our faces, and we say that the wind is rising, but we know not whence it comes, or whither it goes: so does the Spirit of God frequently visit us with strong and holy impulses. There is a divine restlessness; a noble discontent; a hunger created in the heart, which will not be satisfied with the husks on which the swine feed. We cannot always understand ourselves, but it is the Lord saying to us, Arise and depart; for this is not your rest.

There are many kinds of voices in the world, and none of them is without signification; and sometimes it is difficult to know the voice of the Lord. But the more truly we partake of the nature of "His own sheep," the more unerringly shall we detect the voice of the Good Shepherd. If you are not quite sure, wait till you are. It is the Shepherd's business to make His presence and wish understood by the timid and perplexed in His flock. The only necessity is to be willing to do His will so soon as it is clearly seen. If you are in doubt, wait in faith till every other door is shut, and one path only lies open before you, and you are able to say: "He leadeth me in the paths of righteousness for His name's sake."

God's voice to the heart is generally corroborated by the drift of outward circumstances. "Jacob beheld the countenance of Laban, and, behold, it was not towards him as before." For some time their relations had been strained. Ten times in six years had Laban altered the method of computing his wages; and now there were symptoms of open rupture. It is always wise to be on the outlook for any evident symptoms of God's will; and here was one.

It is very bitter to behold a change passing over men and women in their behavior towards us; a change which we cannot avert. We dread it as the timid passenger by the night mail dreads the roar of the waves, as they seethe, white with rage, outside the harbor bar. And yet God is undoubtedly in all this. It is the way which He is taking through the deep. Listen to the Divine assurance, "I am with thee." The Good Shepherd Himself is putting you forth from the warm fold, now almost bare, that He may conduct you to green pastures and living waters. The Master Himself is emptying you from vessel to vessel; lest you should settle on your lees. The Husbandman Himself is exposing you to that painful process of transplanting, which is said to be one of the surest methods of luxuriant growth. Take heart: it is only part of the process of making you a prince; you need it badly enough—in no other way can your mean Jacob-nature be replaced by something better.

II. THE TENACITY OF CIRCUMSTANCES. When the pilgrim spirit essays to obey the voice of God, the house is always filled with neighbors to dissuade from the rash resolve. "As Christian ran, some mocked; others threatened; and some cried after him to return." There was something of this in Jacob's case. The bird-lime clung closely to him, as he began to plume his wings for his homeward flight.

He was evidently afraid that his wives would hinder his return. It would have been natural if they had. Was it likely that they would at once consent to his proposal to tear them from their kindred and land? This fear may have greatly hindered Jacob. He at least thought it necessary to fortify himself with a quiver full of arguments, in order to carry his point. In those arguments we catch another glimpse of his cowardly and crafty nature. They are a strange medley of lies, and cant, and truth. He might have saved himself from all this, if he had only trusted God to roll away the stones from the path of obedience. For God had been at work before him; and had prepared their hearts, so that they at once assented to his plan, saying: "We have no further ties to home; now then, whatsoever God hath said unto thee, do." If we would only go forward in simple obedience, we should find that there would be no need for our diplomacy; He would go before us, making the crooked straight, and the rough smooth.

In the endeavors of Laban to retain Jacob, we have a vivid picture of the eager energy with which the world would retain us, when we are about to turn away from it forever. It pursues us, with all its allies, for seven days and more (v. 23). It asks us why we are not content to abide with it (v. 27). It professes its willingness to make our religion palatable, by mingling with it its own tabret and dance (v. 27). It appeals to our feelings, and asks us not to be too cruel (v. 28). It threatens us (v. 29). It jeers us with our sudden compunction, after so many years of contentment with its company (v. 30). It reproaches us with our inconsistency in making so much of our God, and yet harboring some cunning sin. "Wherefore hast thou stolen my gods?" (v. 30). Ah, friends, how sad it is, when we, who profess so much, give occasion to our foes to sneer, because of the secret idols which they know we carry with us! Sometimes it is not we who are to blame, so much as our Rachels—our wives, or children, or friends. But we should never rest till, as far as we know, our camp is clear of the accursed thing.

At last, our Labans, who would hold us fast, having tried every expedient, content themselves with groaning, "What can I do this day?" Blustering often ends in bewailing over an unalterable destiny.

Thus the heap of witness is raised at length. Oh that you might break away from that life of worldliness in which you have tarried too long! Make a clean break with it! Only do not do it secretly, as Jacob did. Better so, than not at all: but it is mean-spirited and cowardly; it always arouses intenser opposition; and it is not worthy of one whose escort is God Himself. The straightforward and outspoken course—which nails its colors to the mast—is always the easiest, and safest, and best.

A midshipman, who was about to leave the sailor's home, where he had been converted, came to the superintendent on the day of going on board, and asked him to write on a card, in plain bold characters, the words, "I am a Christian." When he was asked his object, he said, "As soon as I get on board, I shall go to my hammock, and put this card where everybody can see it: it will save a lot of trouble; for everyone will know at once which side I am on, and will expect me to keep true to it." This is raising the heap of witness.

Let us raise that heap: let me help you rear it; gather stones, and pile them into the form of that cross by which the world was crucified to St. Paul, and he to the world. Eat there the feast that speaks of life through death. Call your friends to witness your solemn act; above all, call God to witness your resolve—that never again shall the world, the flesh, or the devil, come over to you, or you pass over to them. This is the true Mizpah, of the Lord's watch.

III. THE DIVINE CARE. Well might Jacob have thrilled with joy, as he said to his wives, "The God of my father has been with me." When God is for us, and with us, who can be against us? Blessed is he who is environed by God, and for whom God fights. He must be more than a conqueror. So Jacob found it; and, at the end of his encounter with Laban, he was able to repeat his assurance, that the God of his father had been with him (v. 42).

At the head of his flocks and herds, with wives and children and slaves, he struck across the Euphrates and the desert, at the utmost speed possible to his encumbered march, but God's angels accompanied him. He met their radiant hosts afterwards (32:1). His flight remained unsuspected for three days; then Laban set off with swift camels in pursuit, and overtook them, when still threading their way among the richly wooded and watered hills of Gilead. It was a moment of real danger; and it was then that God interposed. "God came to Laban the Syrian by night." That dream laid an irresistible spell on Laban, which prevented him from carrying out his design to do Jacob hurt.

Jacob was an erring and unworthy child, but God did not leave or forsake him. He does not love us (as we so often falsely tell little children) because we are good, but to make us so. As He does not set His love on us because of our deserts, so He does not turn it away from us because of our sins. He hates our sins, but He loves ourselves with a love that sin can neither wear out, nor turn away. Thus He was able to throw His protection round His erring child; and this was part of the loving discipline which was leading Jacob to a goal of which he never dreamed.

Jacob conceived that he was a model shepherd (v. 38), but he little realized how lovingly he was being protected by the shepherd care of Him who keeps Israel, and who neither slumbers nor sleeps. That protection may be ours.

O Thou, who art the Good Shepherd; who does guard Thy flock, in drought and frost, with untried and unabated tenderness; who does go after that which is gone astray, until Thou does find it, bringing it back upon Thy shoulders—we, too, have gone astray like lost sheep. Seek Thy servants; at whatever cost, disentangle us from the meshes of the world; and take care of us until Thine own ideal is realized in our lives.

9

The Midnight Wrestle

The Sun of Righteousness on me
Hath rose, with healing in His wings.
Withered my nature's strength; from Thee
My soul its life and succor brings;
My help is all laid up above;
Thy nature and Thy name is Love!
Contented now, upon my thigh
I halt, till life's short journey end;
All helplessness, all weakness, I
On Thee alone for strength depend;
Nor have I power from Thee to move:
Thy nature and Thy name is Love!

Genesis 32   Wesley

I n the morning after his interview with Laban, Jacob broke up his camp on the heights of Gilead, and slowly took his journey southwards. He little knew that that day was to be the crisis of his life. "Thou knowest not what a day may bring forth," not of evil only, but of blessing. It may be that this day has been predestined from all eternity to be that of thy transformation from the craft and cunning of years, to a life of subjection to the will of God, and of power over men.

This wondrous scene does not, in my opinion, correspond to that change which we call conversion. That was determined, surely, by the angel vision at Bethel. But it may rather be compared with that further blessing, which sometimes comes to a Christian after some years of religious experience and profession. There is no reason, in the nature of things, why it should be so. There is no reason why, at the moment of conversion, we should not at once step into the realization and enjoyment of all the possibilities of Christian living. But still, as a matter of fact, it very often happens that some years of wilderness wandering do intervene between the deliverance of the Passover and the passage across the Jordan into the land of promise, and rest, and victory. Many a child of God who has no doubt of acceptance and forgiveness, is conscious of a broken and fitful experience: often foiled and overthrown; wishing to do good, but unable to do it; full of self-reproach and bitterness of soul. Then there comes a time when he is almost forced into a new experience. He passes into a climate that brings into glorious fruitage the seed germs which were lying in his nature undeveloped. He receives an abounding freshet of grace, that lifts him sheer above all the former levels of his existence, and launches him on the flood tide of blessedness. If you have never known this in happy experience, you can hardly understand what an extraordinary change comes over all things; or how great a contrast severs the new from the old. Such an experience fell to Jacob's lot after that memorable night.

Three events are narrated in this chapter, corresponding to morning, afternoon, and night of that memorable day.

(1) IN THE MORNING, we are told that the angels of God met him. Those words tremble with mystic and indescribable beauty. How did it befall? Did they come in twos or threes? Or, as he turned some corner in the mountain pass, did he see a long procession of bright harnessed angels, marching four abreast, with golden bands girding about them their lustrous robes, while the music of heaven beat time? Would it not remind him of Bethel, that lay across the chasm of five-and-twenty years? Would it not nerve and prepare him for coming danger?

Doubtless these angel bands are always passing by us; only our eyes are holden so that we do not see them. But whether we see them or not, we may always reckon on their being at hand—especially when some heavy trial is near. "The angel of the Lord encampeth round about them that fear Him, and delivereth them." This is Mahanaim. Here two hosts are meeting; the mountain is full of horses and chariots of fire around us; more are they that are with us than all they which are against us.

(2) As the day wore on to AFTERNOON, Jacob's spirit was shaken to the center by ominous tidings. He had sent messengers, as Arab chiefs would do still, to announce to Esau his return, and to ascertain his mind. They now returned in breathless haste to say that Esau was coming to meet him, with four hundred men at his back. Jacob was panic-

stricken; and well he might be. His all was at stake—wives and children; herds and cattle; the careful gains of six laborious years. The Mizpah tower barred the way back; his bridge was, so to speak, burned behind him. Around him were robber tribes, eager to seize on the rich booty, if he showed the least sign of vacillation or fear. But to go on seemed to involve a risk of inevitable ruin. There was just one alternative—which most men will only turn to when all other expedients have failed: he could at least pray; and to prayer he betook himself. It may have been a long time since he prayed like this.

For years his nobler self had been overgrown by a noxious growth of weeds, and drugged to unconsciousness by the cares of this life; the deceitfulness of riches; and the lusts of many things. The evil conscience cannot pray. Prayer cannot live in the heart with deceit, and craft, and villainy, but passes out unnoticed and unmissed. But now, under the shock of this terrible danger, the olden spirit revived in him; and the hair of consecration began to grow again. (See Num. 6). Is not this the key to God's dealings with us all? He brings us into sore straits; He shuts us up in a corner; He causes the walls and ceiling and floor of our room to draw together, as if to crush us. At such moments there is only one resource left. It is Himself. We must fly to God, to escape from God. We are driven to our knees, with no language but a cry. And though that cry consists mostly of a confession of unworthiness, yet it is enough: the silence is broken; the avenues are cleared of their choking undergrowth; the child has already left the far country, and is on his way home. Was not this the experience of the Syro-Phoenician woman? Her utter misery made her seek Christ; she found Him out in a retirement which would have concealed Him from all save one in her dire need; and His apparent denial drove her to climb an altitude of faith, and to utter words of desperate boldness, from which she would have shrunk except under the pressure of that terrible agony of soul. The love of God is great enough to cause us pain—if only it can force us to positions from which we had heretofore shrunk, but from which we shall never again recede.

There are many healthy symptoms in that prayer. In some respects it may serve as a mold into which our own spirits may pour themselves, when melted in the fiery furnace of sorrow.

He began by quoting God's promise: "Thou saidst." He did so twice (9, 12). Ah, he had got God in his power then! God puts Himself within our reach in His promises; and when we can say to Him, "Thou saidst," He cannot say nay—He must do as He has said. If Herod was so particular for his oath's sake, what will not our God be? Be sure, in prayer, to get your feet well on a promise; it will give you purchase enough to force open the gates of heaven, and to take it by force.

He next went to confession: "I am not worthy." There passed before his mind his deceit to his aged father; his behavior to Esau; his years of trickery to Laban. All the meanness of his heart and life stood revealed, as a landscape is revealed when the midnight sky is riven by the lightning flash. Conscience came forth from its retreat in the dungeons of his nature, and climbed the stairs, and stood in the throne room of his spirit: as Nathan before David; or John the Baptist before Herod; or Paul before Felix, the Roman governor, who trembled as he spake of righteousness, temperance, and judgment to come. And as the sea of memory gave up the dead past to a terrible resurrection, and as it all stood in vivid minuteness before him, was there not plenty to justify his penitent confession?—"I am not worthy." Great soul anguish will generally wring some such cry from our startled and stricken hearts. If there is one position that better becomes us than another, it is that of the publican with downcast eyes; nor can we improve on his prayer, "God be merciful to me, *the* sinner."

Then he passed on to plead for deliverance: "Deliver me, I pray thee, from the hand of my brother, from the hand of Esau." It was, of course, quite right to pray thus, but I cannot feel that it was a wholehearted prayer: for he had hardly finished it, when he reverted to the plan on which he had been busy before he turned aside to pray. Jacob's first thought was always a plan. He had a plan for Isaac's blessing; and another for his property; and now another to appease Esau. Of course, I have no word to say against planning, when that is evidently God's method of delivering us, but I am desperately afraid lest our planning should take the place of simple waiting on God, till the cloud rises, and moves forward, and shows us our path across the trackless sands. We are all so apt to pray, and then to try and concoct a plan for our own deliverance. Surely the nobler attitude is, after prayer, to stand still for

God to develop His plan, leading us in ways that we had never guessed. The blessed life of our Lord was absolutely planless.

There was too much selfhood in Jacob; as there is also in us. This must be broken down, and put in the place of death. The I-life must be crucified before the Christ-life can take its place. The sinews of the old nature must be utterly shriveled; that the new nature, whose only strength is to cling, may be manifested in power. This was the object of that mysterious conflict, which left so deep an impression on Jacob's life.

(3) IT WAS MIDNIGHT. Jacob had already sent across the Jabbok his property, his children, even the beloved Rachel. It seemed as if, amid the awful pressure of that anxiety, he could not bear the noise of the camp; the prattlings of the children; or even the presence of the only woman he ever really loved. "He caused them to pass over the brook; and sent over that he had. And Jacob was left alone." When the soul enters its Gethsemane, it withdraws a stone's cast from its most trusted friends. Around him was the profound stillness of those most desolate regions; beside him the murmur of the rapid brook over the stones; above him the infinite depths of heaven, bejeweled with stars. There, alone, he considered the past; and anticipated the future; and felt the meanness of the aims for which he had sold his soul; and saw the wretched failure of his life: and so, suddenly, he became aware that a mysterious combatant was at his side, drawing him into a conflict, half literal and half spiritual, which lasted till break of day.

Was this a literal contest? There is no reason to deny it. We know that the Son of God sometimes anticipated His incarnation by assuming literal physical shapes. "His delights were of old amongst the sons of men." And it would have been as possible for Him to wrestle literally with Jacob, as for Him to offer His hands to the touch of Thomas after His resurrection. The physical must have been largely present, because, when he resumed his journey, Jacob halted upon his thigh: It was a physical fact; physically commemorated by the Israelites to this day, who abstain from eating of that part in animals which corresponds to the sinew that shrank in Jacob's thigh. Men do not become lame in imaginary conflicts. But, in any case, the outward wrestling was only a poor symbol of the spiritual struggle which convulsed the patriarch's soul; and is as real in the experience of earnest men today as when the world was young.

Remember that the conflict originated not with Jacob, but with the angel: "There wrestled a Man with him." This passage is often quoted as an instance of Jacob's earnestness in prayer. It is nothing of the sort. It is an instance of God's earnestness to take from us all that hinders our truest life; while we resist Him with all our might and main. It was not that Jacob wished to obtain aught from God, but it was that He—the angel Jehovah—had a controversy with this double-dealing and crafty child of His; desirous to break up his self-sufficiency forever; and to give scope for the development of the Israel that lay cramped and coffined within.

There is an illustration of this in the life of Moses. For forty years he lived in the retirement of the desert. At last he set out for Egypt, accompanied by his wife and children. Concerning those children, in deference to their mother's wish, he seems to have neglected a rite, binding, by Divine command, on every son of Abraham. And it came to pass in the way, that the Lord barred his journey, and even threatened him with death, until he had obeyed the injunction he had ignored; then He let him go. So it was with Jacob. There was much in him that needed to be laid aside; much self-sufficiency requiring to be broken down; much dross that had to be burned out by a consuming fire; and so the Love of God drew near to him on that solemn night, to wrest these things from him at whatever cost.

Has not "this Man" that wrestled with Jacob found you out? Have you not felt a holy discontent with yourself? Have you not felt that certain things, long cherished and loved, should be given up, though it should cost you blood? Have you not felt that you should yield your whole being to God, but there has been a rebellious uprising of self-will within you, as if it were impossible for you to make the surrender? Have you not felt in an agony, between the stirrings of God's good Spirit on the one hand, and the preferences of your own choice on the other? Have you not felt as if some mighty power were wrestling with you, against you, and for your good? Surely these convulsive throes; these heaven-born strivings; these mysterious workings—are not of man, or of the will of the flesh, but of God. It is God that works in you, and wrestles with you. Glory be to Him for His tender patience, interest, and love!

At first Jacob held his own. "He saw that he prevailed not against him." The strength that, years before, had rolled the stone from the well for Rachel's sheep, was vigorous yet; and he was in no humor to submit. And thus we do all resist the love of God. We carry out our own plans; we follow our own will; we are strong in our own self-sufficiency. "When thou wast young, thou girdedst thyself, and walkedst whither thou wouldest." Each one of us is dowered with that wonderful power of holding our own against God; and He knows, sorrowfully, that He cannot prevail against us, without taking some severe measures which will give us no alternative but to yield.

Then the angel touched the hollow of his thigh. Whatever it is that enables a soul, whom God designs to bless, to stand out against Him, God will touch. It may be the pride of wealth; or of influence; or of affection, but it will not be spared—God will touch it. It may be something as natural as a sinew, but if it robs a man of spiritual blessing, God will touch it. It may be as small a thing as a sinew, but its influence in making a man strong in his resistance of blessing will be enough to condemn it—and God will touch it. And beneath that touch it will shrink and shrivel; and you will limp to the end of life. Remember that the sinew never shrinks save beneath the touch of the Angel hand—the touch of tender love. This is why your schemes have miscarried; and your children have faded in untimely decay; and your life has been haunted by disappointment. God has touched the sinew of your strength; and it has dried up. Oh, you who are still holding out against Him, make haste to yield, lest some worse thing come upon you!

Then Jacob went from resisting to clinging. As the day broke, the Angel would be gone, but He could not, because Jacob clung to Him with a death grip. The request to be let go indicates how tenaciously the limping patriarch clung to Him for support. He had abandoned the posture of defense and resistance; and had fastened himself on to the Angel—as a terrified child clasps its arms tightly around its father's neck. That is a glad moment in the history of the human spirit, when it throws both arms around the risen Savior; and hangs on Him, and will not let Him go. It is the attitude of blessing. It is the posture of power. It is the sublime condition in which Christ will whisper His own new name, which no man knows saving he that receives it. Have you ever come to this? Have you abandoned the art of self-defense for the artlessness of clinging trust? Have you felt able to rejoice in your inability to stand alone, because it has made the Lord Jesus so real? Have you reached the point of self-surrender? If not, ask God to show you what sinew it is that makes you too strong for Him to bless you; ask Him to touch it, so that you shall be able to hold out no more. And then you will discover the threefold blessing which is yours.

(1) *The changed name.* In olden days, names were given not for euphony, or by caprice, but for character. A man's character was in his name. Now, when Jacob came into the attitude of blessing—an attitude which has two parts: viz.; absolute abandonment of self, and a trust which clings to Christ—then immediately the Angel said, "What is thy name?" And he said, "Jacob. By nature I am a supplanter, a rogue, and a cheat." Never shrink from declaring your true character: "My name is Sinner." "And he said, thy name shall be no more Jacob, but Israel: a prince with God." The changed name indicated a changed character. Jacob was swallowed up of light. He was clothed upon with the name and nature of a prince. There is only one way to princeliness—it is the thorn-set path of self-surrender and of faith. Why should you not now yield yourself entirely to God, and give Him your whole being? It is only a reasonable service: and out if it will spring a tenacity of faith; and a power for service; and a royalty of character—enough to make you willing to bear the limp, which proves that your own strength has passed away forever.

(2) *Power.* The better rendering of these words would be: "As a prince hast thou power with God; and with man thou shalt prevail." We sigh for power—power over ourselves; power for service; power over the principalities of wicked spirits. But before we can receive power with the creature, we must obtain it from the Creator. The man who would have power with men must first have it with God; and we can only get power with God when our own strength has failed, and we limp. "I glory in infirmity, that the power of Christ may rest upon me;

for when I am weak, then am I strong." Oh for the withered sinew of our own strength, that we may lay hold on the strength of God!

(3) *The beatific vision.* "I have seen God face to face." Our moments of vision come at daybreak: but they are ushered in by the agony of dread; the long midnight vigil; the extreme agony of conflict; the shrinking of the sinew. Yet, when they come, they are so glorious, that the frame is almost overpowered with the brightness of that light, and the exceeding weight of glory. The price is dear, but the vision is more than worth it all. The sufferings are not worthy to be compared with the glory revealed.

This is life; a long wrestle against the love of God, which longs to make us royal. As the years go on, we begin to cling where once we struggled; and as the morn of heaven breaks, we catch glimpses of the Angel face of love, and hear His whispered name: and as He blesses us, we awake to find ourselves living, and face to face with God—and that is heaven itself.

❦ 10
Failure

Or sometimes strangely I forget;
And, learning o'er and o'er
A lesson all with teardrops wet,
Which I had learnt before.
He chides me not, but waits awhile;
Then wipes my heavy eyes;
Oh, what a Teacher is our God—
So patient and so wise!

F. R. Havergal

Genesis 33, 34

That midnight wrestle, which last engaged our thoughts, made an epoch in Jacob's life. It was the moment in which he stepped up to a new level in his experience—the level of Israel the prince. But, let us remember, it is one thing to step up to a level like that; it is quite another to keep it. Some, when they touch a new attainment, keep to it, and are blessed forevermore; others, when they have stood there for a moment, recede from it. Yet it is well for them to have stood for even a moment on the shining tablelands, where God Himself is sun: for, when once they have caught sight of a new ideal, they will never be satisfied to live as they have lived; and, even if they do not win it at once as an abiding experience, they will come to it afterwards. Jacob, alas! soon stepped down from that glorious level to which the Angel had lifted him.

This descent is indicated by the retention, in the sacred record, of the name Jacob. We should have expected that it would have been replaced by the new title, Israel—as Abram was by Abraham, but it is not so. How could he be called Israel, when he had so soon reverted to the life of Jacob; and had gone back from the life of clinging, to the

79

cringing, crafty, scheming life which he had been leading all too long? The time will come when Israel shall become his habitual designation, but not yet—not yet. Our Heavenly Father is very tender with us; and if we do not learn His lessons at once, He will present them to us again and again—now in one form, then in another—until at last His ideal is accomplished in our characters and lives.

We have to consider now the three evidences of failure; which are recounted in these chapters.

I. THE FIRST FAILURE WAS IN HIS MANNER OF MEETING ESAU. As the morning broke, "Jacob lifted up his eyes, and looked; and, behold, Esau came, and with him four hundred men." Such is life. It is filled with sharply varied experiences. Now the Angel; then the coming of Esau. Now forty days on the brow of Sinai with God; then the golden calf. Now the Mountain of Transfiguration; then the bitter cross. Now Patmos, with its visions; then the cold grey rock, and the commonplaces of captivity and loneliness.

Yet, how grateful should we be that it is so! Life might have been full of Esaus, and no Jacobs; full of Gethsemanes, and no glimpses into heaven; full of grey commonplaces, and no rapturous visions. The bright days of our lives outnumber the dark ones. There are more sweets than bitters; more smiles than tears; more mercies than miseries.

How often do we find that a great blessing—like that which came to Jacob by the fords of the Jabbok—is sent to prepare us for a great trial. God prevents us, and prepares us, with the blessings of His goodness. He takes us up the Hill Difficulty; into the House Beautiful: where we sleep in the Chamber of Peace, which looks toward the sunrise. Not that we should stay there: but that we should be rested, and accoutered, and prepared to meet Apollyon in the Valley; and to pass unscathed through the Shadow of Death and Vanity Fair. Do not be surprised or discouraged if a time of fiery trial should follow a season of unusual blessing; indeed, you may be rather surprised if it does not. But when it comes, be sure to do as Jacob did not do, and draw heavily upon all those resources of strength and comfort which have been stored up during the previous days of clear shining and peace.

There are two ways of meeting troubles: the one is the way of the flesh; the other, of the Spirit. The flesh anticipates them with terror; prepares against them with trembling hands; prays in a panic, and then cringes before them—as Jacob, who bowed himself to the ground seven times, until he came near his brother. The way of faith is far better. She clings to God; she hears God say, "I am with thee, and will keep thee"; she believes that He will keep His word; she reviews the past, when the hands of Laban were tied, and argues that God can do as much again; she goes to meet trouble, not cringing but erect, sure that God has already been at work in the heart of difficulty: and that, however grim they may seem in the distance, yet the lions are chained, the wolf claws are extracted; and the arrows have been deprived of their barbed tips.

I have always admired the refusal of the members of Lord Elgin's suite to crawl on the ground into the presence of the Emperor of China. When they learned that that was the posture which all foreigners were expected to assume, they indignantly replied that they certainly would not give to the Emperor of China a homage which their own Most Gracious Sovereign did not require; and, in the end, they were permitted to enter his presence erect. This is the natural posture of an Englishman, but it is more surely the native posture of faith.

Some who read this may be dreading a meeting with their Esaus tomorrow: some creditor; some demand for payment; some awkward problem; some difficulty. And you are today worrying, planning, scheming, and contriving, as Jacob did, in arranging his wives, and children, and servants, while tomorrow you will go cringing and creeping towards it.

Listen to a more excellent way. Do not lift up your eyes and look for Esaus. Those who look for troubles will not be long without finding trouble to look at. But lift them higher—to Him from whom our help comes. Then you will be able to meet your troubles with an unperturbed spirit. Those who have seen the face of God need not fear the face of a man that shall die. To have power with God is to have power over all the evils that threaten us.

Besides all this, when prayer has preceded trial, the trial turns out to be much less than we anticipated. The women found, when they reached the sepulcher, that the dreaded stone had been rolled away.

When Peter reached the outer gate, that threatened to be an insurmountable obstacle to liberty, it opened to him of its own accord. So Jacob dreaded that meeting with Esau, but when Esau came up with him, he ran to meet him, and embraced him, and fell on his neck, and kissed him: and they wept. The heroic Gordon used to say that, in his lonely camel rides, he often in prayer encountered and disarmed hostile chiefs, before he rode, unaccompanied, into their presence. None can guess, if they have not tried it for themselves, what a solvent prayer is for the difficulties and agonies of life.

It is very beautiful to see that, in this, God was better to Jacob than his fears, or his faith. While he was foreboding the worst, his heavenly Friend was preparing deliverance; as, years after the Lord stretched out His hand and saved from the yeasty waves the faithless Apostle, who had looked away from Himself to the terrors of the storm.

II. The Second Failure Was in the Subterfuge to Which Jacob Resorted, to Free Himself from Esau's Company. When Esau offered him the protection of his armed men, he was at once in a panic; for he dreaded them even more than the Bedouins of the wilds. He tried to evade the proposal by many excuses; especially explaining that his flocks and his children could not keep up with their more rapid pace. And finally, still further to reconcile Esau to the separation, he promised to come at last to Seir, where Esau had fixed his abode.

Now I do not, for a single moment, believe that Jacob really meant to go to Seir; for as soon as he had seen the rear of Esau's retiring forces, he journeyed in the contrary direction to Succoth. All such subterfuge and lying were utterly unworthy of the man who had seen God's angels face to face.

What wretched failure was here! The bright dawn was all too speedily overcast and clouded; and if it had not been for the marvelous tenderness of God, there is no telling how much further Jacob would have drifted, or how indefinitely distant the day would have been in which he should be worthy to bear the name of Israel.

III. The Third Failure Was in Settling at Shechem. God had not said, Go to Shechem, but, "I am the God of Bethel." Bethel, rather than Shechem, was his appointed goal. But alas! we are all too ready to fall short of God's schemes for our elevation and blessedness. And so Jacob came to Shalem, a city of Shechem.

But he did worse; he pitched his tent before the city—as Lot did when he pitched his tent before Sodom. What took him there? Was it that Rachel persuaded him that a little society would be a pleasant relief to the monotony and seclusion of the camp life? Was it that his children urged him to it against his better mind? Was it some idea of obtaining eligible alliances for his children among the children of the land? Whatever may have been his reason, there stands the sad and solemn fact that Jacob pitched his tent *before the city.*

Are not many Christians doing so still? They live on the edge of the world, just on the borderland; far enough away to justify a religious profession, yet near enough to run into it for sweets. They send their children to fashionable schools, that they may acquire the false veneer of the world, and pass muster in its drawing rooms. They remove into the fashionable quarters of a town; and adopt a certain style; and throw themselves into the swim of all manner of worldly engagements—that they may get in with "society." They choose their Church, their pastimes, their friendships, on the sole principle of doing as others do; and of forming good alliances for their children. What is all this but pitching the tent towards Shechem?

"But what are we to do?" say they; "our children must have society; they cannot be recluses, or be forever shut up in our homes." But why need we cater for them by rushing into the world? Are there not plenty of innocent pastimes, on which worldliness has never breathed its withering breath? Are there not enough elements in the bright social intercourse of the family circle; in the play of imagination and wholesome merriment; in games of skill; in the charms of books; in the recital of travel and adventure; in the witchery of wholesome songs and music; and even in the revelations of modern popular science—to beguile the hours of long winter evenings, without calling in the aid of worldly society, whose brightest hours leave a sense of vacuity and thirst, to say nothing of a positive sting? The most earnest religion does not debar us from manly sports: the swift movement of the skater over the frozen lake; the evening row; the exhilarating climb: or from the culture of the faculties of art; and music; and imagination; of science and poesy. Surely, in all these there is enough to brighten Christian homes, without grieving the Holy Spirit, or lowering their tone. But if parents and guardians will insist on something more exciting and stimulating than these, they must reckon on being called upon to pay the price. They may have the dicebox, the theater, the dance, if they will, but they must learn, by sad experience, the bitter cost. He needs a long spoon who sups with the devil. The fact is, it is much easier to give these things than to arouse oneself to provide something better. The something better needs time and thought; and staying at home from religious meetings, to give it effect: but the ultimate benefit will more than repay the self-denial.

We cannot put old heads on young shoulders; or our experience into young hearts. We must let our children see a brightness in our behavior which shall not repel them from us, but win them to our Savior. But in doing this, it is quite unnecessary to go to those empty cisterns which the children of the world have hewn for themselves, and which yield no water. We may find, with a little trouble, other wells, through which the living water rises with a sparkle and a beauty that cannot fail to attract young hearts not yet spoiled by the world's glamour and show.

But Jacob did still worse. Not content with pitching his tent before the city, he bought the parcel of ground "where he had pitched his tent." Abraham bought a parcel of ground in which to bury his dead; and this was no declension from the pilgrim spirit—it rather placed it in clearer relief. But as Jacob paid down his hundred pieces of money, each of which bore the rude imprint of a lamb, he was abandoning the pilgrim spirit and the pilgrim attitude, and was *buying* that which God had promised to *give* to him and to his seed. The true spirit of faith would have waited quietly, until God had made good His repeated promise.

It may be that Jacob sought to conciliate his conscience by building the altar, and dedicating it to the God of Israel. Or perhaps he thought to counteract the effect of the idolatrous city, by this means. In some such way professing Christians sometimes try to find an antidote for a week of worldliness in the religious observance of the Lord's day. They allow their children to go into the world, but they insist on their attending family worship before they retire to rest. Where the altar and the world are put into rivalry, there is no doubt as to which will win the day: the Shechem gate will appeal too strongly to our natural tendencies; and we shall find ourselves and our children drifting into Shechem—while the grass of neglect grows up around the altar, or it becomes broken down and disused.

"And Dinah, the daughter of Leah, which she bare unto Jacob, went out to see the daughters of the land." It is a startling announcement, but it contains nothing more than might have been expected. Poor girl! A moth fluttering about a flame! A foolish fish nibbling at the bait! Was she lonely, being the only girl? Did she want to show off some piece of jewelry or dress? Did she long for more admiration, or fascinating society, than she could find at home? Was there a secret drawing to the young men of the place? She went along a path, that seemed to her girlish fancy ever so much more attractive than the dull routine of home. She took no heed to the warnings that may have been addressed to her. And it all ended—as it has ended in thousands of cases since—in misery, ruin, and unutterable disgrace.

She was kindly received. The world will always give a hearty welcome to those who bear a Christian name. Perhaps there is a sense of relief in feeling that it cannot be so bad after all, since Christians do not hesitate to take part with it. The welcome and "well-done" of worldly men should always put us on our guard. "What evil thing have I done," said a shrewd observer, "that yonder worldling speaks so well of me?"

She fascinated the young prince, and fell. It is the old, old story, which is ever new. On the one hand—rank, and wealth, and unbridled appetite; on the other—beauty, weakness, and dallying with temptation. But to whom was her fall due? To Shechem? Yes. To herself? Yes. But, also to Jacob. He must forever reproach himself for his daughter's murdered innocence. But of what use were his reproaches when the deed was done; and the honor of his house was gone; and his name stank among the inhabitants of the land? Would that some Christian parents, reading these words, might take warning as to the end of a pathway on which they are encouraging their children to tread! To stay now may save them tears of blood, and years of fruitless agony. In the strongest terms, let me entreat them not to play on the rim of the whirlpool: lest its hurrying waters catch the too-hazardous craft before they are aware; and whirl them round in an ever giddier dance; and finally engulf them in its eddying vortex.

And all this came because Jacob stepped down from the Israel level back to his old unlovely self. Not improbably you, my reader, have done the same. You have attended meetings which had stirred you to the very depths; and beneath their spell you have thought that life could never be the same again, but that the common round of daily duty would be radiant with the lingering glory of the Transfiguration Mount. You have even gone further: at the Jabbok ford you have met with the Angel Jehovah, the sinew of your strength has shrunk beneath His touch, and you have bent beneath the blessing of His hand. But, notwithstanding all, you have stepped back and down into the old low-level life. You wonder how you were ever so mightily affected, and why the whole experience has faded from you, as some radiant glory which for a moment shone in the western sky, but has died away into dusky twilight.

Let us understand the causes of this relapse, and see how we may guard against its recurrence.

It arises, first, from trusting in the impulse received at a given moment, as though that were sufficient to carry the soul forward through all coming days; and there is, therefore, a relaxation of watchfulness, and prayer, and Bible study. We are all so apt to substitute an experience for abiding fellowship with the Son of God; to dwell in the past, instead of in the living present; to take out the dry and moldy manna we gathered yesterday, instead of being on the alert in the early dawn to get new manna fresh from its baptism of dew. This mistake in Christian experience can only be obviated by careful cultivation of the daily, hourly, friendship of the living Savior. And even this cannot be attained by any effort or resolution of our own, but by the grace of the Holy Spirit, who alone can teach us the art of daily abiding.

Secondly, it may arise from the energy of the self life, which the Apostle Paul calls *the flesh*. Before regeneration we attempt to justify ourselves; being regenerate, we attempt to sanctify ourselves. At meetings of consecration, well-meaning persons endeavor to consecrate themselves. In each case, the element of self makes every effort abortive. We can no more consecrate, in the deepest meaning of that word, than we can justify ourselves. God must be all in all. Let us ask Him to take, keep, and seal us, by the Holy Ghost. There must be more of God in our lives. We must speak less of God helping us, and more of His performing all things for us, as He did for the Psalmist.

Thirdly, these failures arise because we are conscious of the subsidence of the keen emotions which once filled our hearts, and suppose that in losing these we have really lost that spiritual attitude which we then assumed. It can never be too often repeated that all the deepest experiences in Christian life consist in acts of the will, which may or may not be accompanied by emotion, and which remain when the glow of feeling has passed. It would not do for us to live in perpetual sunshine, nor in unbroken rapture; we should be exhausted by an overexpenditure of the vital forces of our souls. God, therefore, withdraws the life of emotion that He may train us to live by faith, and in our wills. We must dare to believe that the blessed experience has not gone, if we can look up to heaven and say, "I *will* to be as I was in the glad hours that bore me to a higher level than any before attained."

Whatever failure comes may also be associated with our reluctance to confess to others the blessing which has irradiated our inner life. It is not necessary to unbare the deepest exercises of our souls to every passerby, but we should not hesitate to confess with our mouth that Jesus Christ is Lord, and tell those with whom we are most intimate what great things the Lord has done for us. To withhold confession, is often to staunch the flow of blessing.

If you are conscious of having failed in any of these respects, ask to be forgiven and restored; put back just where you were; and trust Him, who is the keeper of the faithful soul, to hold you as a star in His right hand, and to trim you as the light of the sacred temple lamps.

✱ 11

Back to Bethel

O God, man's heart is darkened,
He will not understand!
Show him Thy cloud and fire;
And, with Thine own right hand
Then lead him through his desert,
Back to Thy Holy Land!
E. A. Procter

Genesis 35

In itself, Bethel was not much. Imagine a long range of broken hills running north and south. The eastern slopes, bleak and tempest riven, descend to the Jordan. The western slopes lie towards the more thickly-peopled parts of Palestine. In the valley at their foot runs the main thoroughfare of Palestine, which has been trodden by centuries of travelers—a rough, broken mountain roadway, following the uneven course of the valley, and intersected by innumerable watercourses. From this track and upwards the mountain slopes are strewn with large sheets of bare rocks—most prone as gravestones, some erect as Druid cromlechs. No house is within sight; no cultivated lands break the stretch of mountain pasture; no domestic animals share the rule of the eagle, the wild goat, and the rabbit.

But to Jacob, Bethel was the most memorable and sacred spot in all the earth. It was there, on the first night of his flight from home, that the mystic ladder had seemed to link earth to heaven, thronged by angels engaged in holy ministry.

Many years had passed since then—years of searching discipline, which had revealed the meanness, the craft, the weakness of his nature.

89

He had fallen far below the promise of his early vows; his better nature had held but a spasmodic supremacy over his worse; even the angel wrestle had only momentarily lifted him to the level of Israel, the Prince. And of late it would seem that even worse symptoms had begun to show themselves. His life at the gate of Shechem had done much to lower his standard and aims; and to assimilate them to those of the people with whom he had been associated. He seems even to have winked at the idols which were in common request among his people, and of the presence of which he was perfectly well aware. There had been a time when, if his dearest wife wished for graven images, she must have them surreptitiously, but now he had become so lax himself, that there was no need for concealment on the part of any (v. 2). Alas! what a fall was this for the man who had built so many altars to Jehovah; and was the chosen depository of those truths for which the world was waiting! For the world's sake, and for his own, it was essential that he should be compelled to regain the ground which he had so grievously lost. It was then that he said to his household, "Let us arise, and go up to Bethel."

This impulse was natural. The emigrant who lives in the soft Bermudas, or in a Canadian log house, as he reaches mature life, will find a strange yearning rising within him for the Highland glen in which he was born. He sends many a longing look towards the Northern stars; and at last starts on pilgrimage. He may find the scene desolate and deserted; yet he is not wholly disappointed: he needed the glut of reality to satisfy the long fever of his soul. It was something like this that came to Jacob. A voice (shall I not call it an instinct, within him?) cried: Go and dwell for a season at Bethel; gaze once more on the familiar scene; put your head down again upon that stone which you set up for a pillar; and review the way in which the Lord thy God hath led thee.

But his untoward circumstances gave a yet further reason. He was in terrible trouble. He had settled himself down, and sunk a well for his supply, which became so famous as to be known through all succeeding time as Jacob's Well; he was intimately identified for several uneventful years with the life of the locality; and then his sons had made his name stink among the inhabitants of the land, by the frenzied passion with which they had revenged their sister's dishonor. He was in imminent danger of destruction from the infuriated tribes around him. He must go somewhere; and it was at this moment that the impulse came to him to go up to Bethel. He might not have heeded it, if the waters of earthly comfort had sufficed for his urgent need. But now that they threatened to fail, and even to turn to poison, he was the more ready to try what Bethel might afford of comfort and safety, of satisfaction and restoration. A drying well will often lead the spirit to the river that flows from the throne of the Lamb.

But, above all, that impulse originated in God Himself, "God said unto Jacob, Arise, go up to Bethel, and dwell there." No human ear now catches the tones of that majestic voice. Yet, God often speaks to us also—through our own consciousness, and within our own souls. Yes, and He speaks more often than most of us are aware. We do not always distinguish the voice within us to be the voice of God. We act on an impulse, we know not why. But as we review our path from the sweet summit of religious revival to which we have been led, we recognize, with thankful awe, that the voice to which we listened was none other than that voice which Jacob first heard speaking to him in his angel-haunted sleep. Has it not been so with you? You have followed an inward impulse, not knowing whence it came, or whither it led; you have wandered blindly on, reaching positions of which you had never dreamed, but which are evidently your special sphere: and it is only on looking backwards that you realize how every step of your way has been ordered by a wisdom not your own; how the impulse originated in Him who prompts the swallows to follow the sun to warmer climes; and how the voice that called you was the voice of God.

But there is something better than this blind obedience, and it would be a happy thing if every child of God had reached it. God is always speaking to us in the incidents of daily life; He has a meaning, and transmits to us a message, in everything which He permits to happen. We are wise, therefore, when we set ourselves to decipher the hieroglyphics in which His meaning is enwrapped; and to question each event as to the tidings which He has entrusted it to bring. We are wiser still, when we lovingly, yea joyfully, accept, and unquestioningly obey.

And why did God wish Jacob to go back to Bethel? Because Bethel was associated with one of the most blessed spiritual experiences of his life. And the summons to go back to Bethel was equivalent to an invitation to return to that fervor, that devotion, and those holy vows, which had made that bare mountain pass the very house of God and the gate of heaven. "Come back; and be as near to Me as you were when you first set up that stone, and annointed it with oil."

There are some words which cannot be spoken in our ears without arousing in us an immediate and touching response. They come on us as a strain of music; or a whiff of perfume on the summer breeze—awakening far-off memories, and exciting emotions long gone by. So must the word *Bethel* have sounded in the ear of Jacob: stirring all his better nature—bidding it arise, and come forth from its long death sleep; and lighting up the nobler spirit of his life. It met with an instant response: "Then Jacob said unto his household, and to all that were with him, Put away the strange gods that are among you; and be clean, and change your garments. And let us arise, and go up to Bethel."

And so he came to Bethel, protected by God's watchful care; and he built there an altar, and God appeared unto him again.

I. MANY CHRISTIANS ARE SUFFERING FROM SPIRITUAL DECLENSION. They hardly realize it, it has crept on them so quietly, but they have drifted far away from their Bethel and Peniel. Grey hairs are on a man before he knows. Summer fruit is beginning to rot within, long before its surface is pitted with specks. The leaf's connection with the branch is severed, even when it looks green. The devil is too shrewd to make Judases at a stroke; he wins us from the side of Christ by hair breadths. We would never think of letting in the lion, but we spare the little foxes, which break down the hedge—through which the lion comes presently. We would never think of letting Delilah cut off our seven locks of hair, but we do no so much object to her binding it with her green withes, though she will creep on to the other. So insensible have you been slipping back; until you are infinitely farther from God than you were in the sacred, happy days that are past.

II. IDOLS ARE THE INEVITABLE SYMPTOM OF INCIPIENT DECAY. Go at autumn into the woods, and see how the members of the fungus tribes are scattered plentifully throughout the unfrequented glades. All through the long scorching summer days their germs were present in the soil, but they were kept from germinating by the dryness of the air, and the heat of the sun. However, there is now nothing to prevent it; nay, the dank damp of decay is the very food of their life. Where the shade is deepest, and the soil most impregnated with the products of corruption, they love to pitch their tents. Wherever, therefore, you find these fungus growths, you may be sure that there is corruption and decay. Similarly, whenever there has set in upon the spiritual life the autumn of decay, you will be sure to find a fungus growth of idols—the sorrowful symptoms that the bright summer time has passed, or is passing away from the soul.

You may hide your idols, like Rachel, but they will not remain hidden: they will work their way forward, until what was hidden as a sin becomes paraded as a boast. It may be that some backslider shall read these lines, conscious that things are not now what they were between him and God. Such a one will bear witness from his own bitter experience, that in proportion to the decay of the inner life there has been the growth of some idol love. You have set your heart on making a reputation, or a fortune; you have loved some worthless friend with an inordinate affection; you have lavished yourself on something or someone outside of God—and as your energies have waxed in this direction, they have waned in the other. "No man can serve two masters: either he will love the one, and hate the other; or else he will hold to the one, and despise the other."

III. THESE IDOLS MUST BE SURRENDERED BEFORE THERE CAN BE VICTORY OR PEACE.

The reason for Jacob's flight before those alien tribes was, of course, the censurable and merciless action of his sons, but above and beyond this, lay the fact that Jacob had been giving some measure of countenance to the existence of idolatry in the camp. I always find, in Christian experience, that failure and defeat indicate the presence of some idol somewhere, and the need of more complete consecration to God. It may be a hidden idol; and it may be hidden by the Rachel of your heart, lovely and beloved: but if it be there, it will be the certain cause of disappointment. You say that you do not find yourself able to overcome besetting sin; that you are tripped up before you look to Christ; that you are sometimes hot as juniper coals, and then cold as ice; you talk about your experience as if Christ had failed—no such thing! Get down on your knees; search out the idols; ransack all the camel baggage, in spite of all that Rachel may say bring out the accursed things, and bury them. Put away the garments spotted with the flesh; only thus will you enter upon the life of victory, or will God appear unto you again.

How wise it was for Jacob to bury those idols right away! If he had kept or carried them with him, he might have been tempted to bring them out again. It was so much better to leave them right there, under the oak in Shechem, before he started for Bethel. I do not think he could have counted on God's delivering care, if he had not acted with such promptness and decision. God would not have been the escort of a pack of idols! Burn the books that have polluted your mind. Cut off the hand that has made you offend. Renounce the drink that has obtained such a power over you; and pour the contents of your cellars down the gutter, lest you be tempted to return to them again. Burn your bridge behind you. Hide the idols under the oak. "Mother," said a betting man, "I have taken the first step to Christianity; I have burned my betting books." We cannot be surprised at the mighty work of God in Ephesus after the splendid *auto-da-fé* that took place in the marketplace (Acts 19:19).

What a man is, that in most cases his family will also be. When Jacob's camp saw that he was himself in earnest, they gave him all the strange gods that were in their hand, and all the earrings that were in their ears. What a solemn responsibility rests on us all in our family life, that we should not, by our silence, connive at either follies or sins. If those around us see that we are consistent and determined, they will not let us go to heaven alone. Christiana and her children will sooner or later follow Christian. "Jacob came to Luz that is, Bethel, he and *all the people that were with him.*"

This, then, is our closing message: put away your idols, and get back to Bethel. Repent, and do the first works. Pray as you used to pray. Study the Bible as you used to study it. Spend the Lord's day as you used to spend it. Build an altar now on the same site on which you built it years ago. Give yourself again to God. True, a sad life of wasted opportunities lies behind you, but do not waste more time in fruitless regrets. Forget the things that are behind; stretch forward to those that are before. And God will appear to you again; and will renew the Princely Name and the Princely Blessing to which you might have thought that you had forfeited all right; moreover, He will promise you marvelous fruitfulness in service, and far-reaching possessions in the Land of promise (vv. 11, 12). All these things are in store for you—if only you will bury your idols, and go up to Bethel, and dwell there. "Goodness and mercy shall follow you all the days of your life; and you shall dwell in the house of the Lord forever." "Return, ye backsliding children; and I will heal your backslidings. Behold, we come unto Thee; for Thou art the Lord our God."

The School of Sorrow

The ills we see—
The mysteries of sorrow deep and long,
The dark enigmas of permitted wrong—
Have all one key:
This strange, sad world is but our Father's school;
All chance and change His love shall grandly overrule.
                                    F. R. Havergal

Genesis 35—42

In manufactories of chinaware there are processes which illustrate our lives with startling force and beauty. Among others which read us deep and helpful lessons, is the burning in of the colors, which had been previously painted on the ware. It is only the skilled hand that can delineate those designs which delight our fancy, but no skill of the painter could make them other than evanescent, unless there were some other method of rendering them permanent. This is accomplished by placing the newly-painted ware in a kiln or furnace, where it is exposed to very intense heat; and the colors are burned in and fixed.

It is very often thus that God makes permanent some great blessing which we have received. He burns it in by placing us amid the fires of keen suffering and sorrow. So often have I noticed this, that I am never surprised to hear men date an unusual amount of trial from the moment in which heaven seemed nearer, and Christ dearer, than ever before. It must be so: or the blessing which they had obtained would fade from their soul—as the tints of sunset fade off earth and sky; or as the photograph fades from the plate, unless it has been "fixed" in the dark chamber. In this respect, there is a precise analogy between the experience of Jacob and ourselves: teaching us again that spiritual life is one, though severed by the centuries; and that the Bible is evidently the Word of God, because it is so certainly the book of man.

When, having left his idols behind, Jacob had got back to Bethel, and had built again the altar of renewed consecration, we are told significantly that "God appeared unto him again, and blessed him." Are all the readers of these lines conscious that the blessing of the Almighty is resting upon them—as the light of the transfigured body of our Lord fell upon the virgin snows of Hermon, and made the darkness light? Has God revealed Himself to you again, after the long, sad lapse of fellowship and communion? Is the backslider back again in the house of God, and at the gate of heaven? If not, would it not be wise to do as Jacob did? Ask God to show you what your idols are. Tell Him that you want to be only, always, all for Him. Put away not only your sins, but your weights—*i.e.,* aught that hinders you in the Christian race. If you cannot do this yourself, tell Him that you are willing for Him to take them from you. If you cannot say that you are willing, tell Him that you are willing to be made willing. And when you have thus surrendered your will, give yourself again to Him; entreat Him to take full possession of your entire being; ally yourself as an Isaac upon the altar of self-dedication; and remember that He takes all we give, and at the moment of our giving it. It may be that He will appear to us at once, flooding our spirits with the old unspeakable joy; or He may keep us waiting for a little. But it matters comparatively little, if only we can say, with the assurance of an unwavering faith, "We are His; nothing shall henceforth separate us from the love of God."

It was a great blessing, indeed, that God vouchsafed to Jacob. "God said unto him, Thy name is Jacob: thy name shall not be called any more Jacob, but Israel shall be thy name." The angel had said as much as this at Peniel; and, for a brief moment, he had shone in the transfiguring gleam of royalty. But the gleam was transient enough; like that which sometimes breaks for a moment far out upon a stormy sea, and is instantly veiled again. But there had been wrought on him a deep spiritual change since then; and his experience had been brought into more constant conformity with the level of Israel, the Prince—which was not reaffirmed as his perpetual designation. And forthwith he was plunged into a fiery furnace of trial, which made both name and character permanent.

But this was not all: God constituted him father of nations and kings; and promised to give to him the land in which he was a wanderer, as his fathers before him. Now these two items of fruitfulness and possession are only possible to those who have passed through the school of suffering. It is in soul travail that our children are born; and it is through much tribulation that we enter into the Kingdom. Let no man think that he can win the highest spiritual attainments without paying the price for them. Our Lord could only be perfected as our Captain and High Priest by the things that He suffered; through His sufferings He became the Author of eternal salvation to all who believe.

We need not dwell further, then, on the probable reasons why, from this moment, Jacob's path was draped in the gathering shadows of outward sorrow. But we may notice what those shadows were. And we may interest ourselves in remarking how, as the sorrows gathered, there was a fuller life, and fruitfulness, and royalty. Jacob is increasingly replaced by Israel, the Prince. Does it not remind us forcibly of another, who said, "Though our outward man perish, the inward man is renewed day by day?" (2 Cor. 4:16). Our affliction is light, and for a moment, compared with the weight of glory which it is working out.

There are four burials in one chapter (Gen. 35), including that of the idols in Shechem. These were the beginning of sorrows.

First, Deborah died; the old favorite nurse, who had accompanied her young mistress, when, long years before, she had left her home across the Euphrates to become Isaac's bride. What a link she must have been with that sacred past! What stories she could tell of the glory of that camp presided over by Abraham, the friend of God! And often she would live again in the past, and tell how bitterly Rebekah rued the fatal advice she gave to her favorite son—whom she was never to see again; and for lack of whom she pined, until she drooped in death, while he still tarried across the distant Euphrates' flood. Rebekah's death may have made the camp of Isaac distasteful to the faithful old servant; and she took the first opportunity of coming to spend her remaining days with him whom, in memory of the long past, she too loved with the tenacious affection of her race. It must have been a sad wrench to Jacob to lay the remains of his mother's closest friend beneath that oak in Bethel. The grief occasioned by her death was evidently quite unusual; since even the oak became known, in after years, as "the oak of tears."

But a worse sorrow was in store. They journeyed from Bethel, and there was but a little way to come to Ephrath. The foremost ranks of the march were already in sight of the hostelry, and were eagerly pressing on for the camping ground. But suddenly a summons from the rear bade them halt. The beloved Rachel cannot go another step. The tidings of her extreme agony and peril silence the motley groups of drovers and slaves, and servants and sons. Gathered in confusion upon the road, they await the issue with the dread suspense which breathlessly marks each flicker of life's taper. That scene would never be forgotten by any of them, least of all by Jacob. When he, too, lay upon his dying bed, in that hieroglyphed Egyptian chamber, it came back to him, with touching force and pathos, such as told the freshness of the wound, and the anguish of the grief, which thirty years could not dull. Ah, sorrow! nature may cast its mantle of greenery over her scars, and golden grain may stand in serried ranks upon the field of Waterloo, but thou can inflict wounds which never seam together, but gape, and gape.

But all the agony of those devoted hearts could not stay that departing spirit: the mother only lived long enough to see her second babe, and to enshrine her sorrow in its name; and then she died, and was buried there in the way to Ephrath, which is Bethlehem. It was a matter of evident regret to Jacob, in after years, that she did not lie, with the rest of her kin, in Machpelah's ancient cave, but he could never forget that lone spot on the way to Ephrath (48:7). And when the wheel of time had brought many changes, and that spot had become famous as the birthplace of the great son of Jesse, still it seemed to the anointed ear of the prophet as if Rachel's spirit haunted the spot, wailing for her children. And even to this day travelers turn aside to visit Rachel's tomb.

Yet another heart pang was measured out to that much-tried man. We suffer keenly through the sins of those we love; and when the father saw his Reuben and his Judah stained with the soil of nameless impurity, he drank perhaps the bitterest cup of his life.

Nor was this all. He lived to see dissension and hatred rend his home. The elder brethren envied and hated their younger brother, Joseph; the son of the beloved Rachel, and the child of his old age. His partiality most certainly added fuel to the flame. It was a great mistake to confer the costly coat that indicated the heir and prince of an Eastern clan. But we can easily understand how naturally the old man would turn to the promising lad, whose dreams bespoke his regal future, and reminded him of his own. "His brethren envied him, but his father observed the saying."

But there was worse to follow. One day the sons brought home the coat he knew so well, but it was daubed with blood, and stained. "This have we found; know now whether it be thy sons' coat or not." It may be that a suspicion even then crossed his mind that there had been foul play. But if it did, he kept it to himself, and only let it slip afterwards in the bitterness of his grief (42:36). He at least professed to believe that an evil beast had devoured the beloved body, and that Joseph had been rent in pieces. How he mourned only those know who have passed through similar anguish. The father's grief touched unwonted chords in the hearts of his children. They rose up to comfort him. "But he refused to be comforted; and said, I will go down to the grave unto my son mourning. Thus his father wept for him."

But another sorrow was in store. Jacob was next called upon to see his aged father breathe his last; and perhaps once more to hear those trembling lips pronounce the blessing which had cost so much. "Isaac gave up the ghost and died, and was gathered unto his people." He joined the great gathering of his clan, in the ranks of which are numbered all meek and true-hearted souls. Who are *our* people, to whom *we* shall be one day gathered? And the two sons buried him. Esau came from Edom—the successful man of the world, who had anticipated this moment years before, as likely to suit his purpose for slaying Jacob, but who was sweetened and softened by the mellowing influence of time. And Jacob, limping in his step; broken by hard toils; stricken by his recent losses—came to help him. There they stood for a moment: the twins whose lives had been such a struggle and such a contrast, reconciled in the presence of the great silence of the grave; and soon to take their several ways, never again to meet, but to tread ever diverging paths, both they and their children, and their children's children. We link hands with the playmates and companions of early life across the tiny stream, and for some distance we can keep them linked, albeit that the streamlet widens between us; then loosing hands, we walk side by side, keeping each other well in view, and talking merrily: but, at last, the mighty river spreads its volume between us; and we can neither see nor hear anything, save the break of the sea upon the shore. It is all important that those who love should be on the same right side of the stream, if they would escape an eternal separation.

On the heels of bereavement came one of those terrific famines to which Eastern countries are subject, and which sweep them bare of people. The family of Jacob was not exempt. The sons seem to have sat down in the stolid indifference born of long privation; and were only aroused by their father's appeal, "Why do ye look one upon another?" They went down into Egypt—in all ages the granary of the world; and after an agonizing interval of suspense returned. But Simeon was not with them; and to get him, and more corn, Jacob must risk the son of his right hand—the lad who had cost him so much in Rachel's death. Who does not sympathize with the cry of agony wrung from that quivering heart, a cry that revealed that depth of love of which it was capable? "Me have ye bereaved of my children: Joseph is not, and Simeon is not; and ye will take Benjamin away: all these things are against me. Ye shall bring down my grey hairs with sorrow to the grave."

In addition to all this, there was growing upon him a sense that his life was closing; that his strength was failing; and that he must prepare to follow his father into the unseen. His years had been few in comparison with those of his forefathers; and he had the weary sense of failure, in that he had "not attained" (47:9). It is a pitiful thing, when an old man finds life ebbing fast away from him; while all his regrets cannot recall one single mistake, or give him the consciousness of having done all he could. Such sorrows fell to Jacob's lot: they fall to our lot still; and when they do, let us learn how to behave ourselves.

I. DO NOT JUDGE BY APPEARANCE. Jacob said, "*All* these things are against me." It was a great mistake. Joseph was alive—the governor of Egypt; sent there to preserve their lives, and to be the stay of his closing years. Simeon was also alive—the blessed link which was drawing and compelling his brothers to return into the presence of the strange Egyptian governor. Benjamin would come safely back again. All things, so far from being against him, were working together for good to him; and if only he would trust God, he would live to see it so. All things are yours, if you are Christ's. All things serve you. Even those that seem most awry and trying are really promoting your best interests. If you knew as much about them as God does, you would go down on your bended knees and thank Him, with streaming eyes, for the most untoward of your circumstances. The seed buried in the ground may rejoice in the frost as much as in the genial sunshine. And even though some events cut us to the quick, if we believe that the infinite love of God is working in and through them, we may sing as Paul and Silas did, albeit that our feet are fast in the stocks. Let us cultivate the habit of looking at the bright side of things. If there are only a few clouds floating in your sky, do not say that the whole is overcast; and if all the heaven is covered, save one small chink of blue, make much of that; and by all means do not exaggerate the darkness.

II. BE SURE THAT GOD HAS A PURPOSE IN ALL YOUR SORROW. The apparent aimlessness of some kinds of pain is sometimes their sorest ingredient. We can suffer more cheerfully if we can clearly see the end which is being slowly reached. But if we cannot, it is hard to lie still and be at rest. But the believer knows that nothing can come to him, save by the permission of God's love. Every trial must reach him through the mystic barriers that engird him; and must show a permit signed by the hand of God Himself. Nothing comes by chance, or by the will of friend or foe, but all is under law. And each several calamity has a specific purpose. "Fitches are not threshed with a sharp threshing instrument, neither is a cartwheel turned about upon the cummin, but the fitches are beaten out with a staff, and the cummin with a rod."

And as the farmer carefully adjusts his method to various kinds of grain, and to accomplish the object he has at heart, so the Almighty varies his method of dealing with us: He ever selects the precise trial that will soonest and best accomplish His purposes; and He only continues it long enough to do all that needs to be done. "Bread corn is bruised: but He will not ever be threshing it; nor break it with the wheel of his cart; nor bruise it with his horsemen." I commend that precious promise to those who think their sorrows past endurance. They will not last forever; they will be suited to our peculiar needs and strength. They will accomplish that on which the great Husbandman has set His heart.

III. REMEMBER THAT NOTHING CAN SEPARATE YOU FROM THE LOVE OF GOD. When Jacob reviewed these dark passages of his life from the serene heights of his dying bed, he saw—as he had never seen it before—that God had shepherded him all his life long; and His Angel had redeemed him from all evil (48:15, 16). We do not realize this at the time: but there is never an experience in life without the watch of that unsleeping Shepherd-eye; never a peril without the interposition of that untiring Shepherd hand. The hand of the Good Physician is ever on the pulse, as we pass through the operation. "Who shall separate us from the love of Christ? Shall tribulation, or distress, or persecution, or famine, or nakedness, or peril, or sword? Nay." These things may sever God from our eyes, and shut away the realization of His love, but they cannot make Him cease to love us; or hide us from Him; or separate us from Him. Take heart, you who are descending into the dark valley of shadow; the Good Shepherd is going at your side, though you see Him not. His rod and staff shall comfort you: yea, His own voice shall speak comfortably to you. Fear not!

IV. ANTICIPATE THE "AFTERWARD." Look not at the things which are seen, but at those which are not seen. Cast into the one scale your sorrows, if you will, but put into the other the glory which shall presently be the outcome of the pain. Consider how splendid it will be, when the discipline is over; and the lovely shape is acquired; and the lesson learned; and the pattern fixed forever. Anticipate the time when every vestige of Jacob shall have been laid aside, and Israel is become the befitting title for your soul. Will not that repay you—because you will have been brought into a oneness with Christ which shall be heaven in miniature?

Take heart, thou bit of heaven's porcelain: thou must be shaped and fashioned on the rapid wheel; thy fairest hues must be burnt in amid the most fiery trials—but thou shalt yet grace the table of thy King; and shalt be used of Him for His choicest purposes.

"Wherefore, let them that suffer according to the will of God, commit the keeping of their souls to Him, as unto a faithful Creator" (1 Pet. 4:19).

❧ 13
Glimpses
of the Israel-Nature

I held it truth with him who sings
To one clear harp in diverse tones,
That men may rise on stepping stones
Of their dead selves to higher things.
Tennyson

Genesis 47

A s a brook runs, it clears itself. It was so with Jacob's life. The discipline of life, like a refining fire, did not fail in its purpose. The dross of his nature was at last well nigh worked out; and the nobler Israel nature became more and more apparent. This change is marked by the change in the name by which he is designated on the inspired page. The old term, Jacob, is used but sparingly; and for the most part Israel is the title of his nobility.

Before we can study the traces of his increasing princeliness of character, we should do well to notice that the name Jacob, though used sparingly, is not wholly dropped. We can never forget what we were. We can never forget what we might be, were it not for the restraining grace of God. I cannot agree with those who think that the Jacob nature may be expunged, wiped out from our being. In my judgment, both Scripture and experience are dead against them. "The flesh lusteth against the Spirit"; and will lust, though with ever decreasing force, unto the end. But it is my joyful belief, also, that "the Spirit lusteth against the flesh"; and represses it with such growing power that it is reduced to the last extremity: and we are kept from doing the things that we otherwise would. Indeed, the self-life can scarcely be said to live, since it makes but the faintest response to temptation. If only we walk in the Spirit, and live in the Spirit, and are led by the Spirit, we shall not fulfill the lusts of the flesh: we shall hardly be aware of their presence in our being; we shall be as good as dead to them. But, in the moment that we cease to abide in living union with the Blessed Spirit, we shall find that the old nature will revive again, in horrid resurrection; and will sweep us down to a sin like that which blackened and saddened all David's later years.

Germs of disease may be constantly breeding in an infected house, but, so long as the disinfecting fluid is well sprinkled on the floors and pendant sheets, they are killed off as soon as they are formed. So sin, though present in the heart, may be choked off, so as to be almost unperceived, because the Holy Ghost is ever at work acting as a disinfectant: but, so soon as His grace is withdrawn, sin regains its old deadly sway, and breathes forth its pestilential poison. It is of the utmost importance, then, to keep in with the Holy Ghost.

One more illustration, though some may deem it far-fetched, will clench and illustrate my meaning. A mesmerist may weave a spell, by passing hands over a man of weaker mind, so as to cast him into all the appearances of death. But he is not dead; and when the charm is broken, the processes of life resume their course. So, beneath the spell of the grace of God's Holy Spirit, our evil self life may lie as dead, only giving faint signs of life; and yet, if that spell be spoken, it will spring up with robust and deadly vigor. It becomes us then to watch and pray, lest we enter into temptation.

There is a beautiful experiment, which the readers of these lines may try for themselves; and which will give them a vivid idea of how the law of the Spirit of life in Christ Jesus can make them free from the law of sin and death. If you take a heavy book and hold it at arm's length, the pull of the law of gravitation will soon draw it downwards, but if some friend will pour down that arm a constant stream of electricity, the flow of the electric current will set you free from the effect of the downward pull. It will still be there, though you will have become almost unconscious of it. Thus it will be when we are filled by the Spirit of God: the downward tendency may be in us yet, but it will be more than counteracted by the habit of that new life, in which the power of the living Savior is ever at work, through the grace of the Holy Ghost.

In the earlier stages of the Christian life, the habit of abiding ever in communion with the Spirit of God is difficult to form and maintain. Some seem to acquire it more habitually and unbrokenly than others. Where this is the case, the Jacob-nature begins to disappear with a suddenness that reminds us of a rapid thaw, which, in a single night, may rid the streets of tons of snow. In the case of those who learn the sweet lesson of unbroken fellowship more slowly, the Jacob-nature keeps breaking in upon the Israel-life as the underlying rock strata will break up through the green sward of a highland valley. Yet, as the years pass on, and the habit of fellowship becomes a permanent possession, these eruptions become less and less frequent; so that at last the Israel-nature has the almost undisputed sway in the life.

We have to notice some manifestations of this Israel-nature in Jacob, like the outshinings of the sun; which, in the early morning, has fought with heavy mists for his supremacy, but at last shines out in a cloudless sky, and sets in radiant glory.

For more than twenty years Jacob mourned for Joseph as dead. The monotony of those years was only broken by new misfortunes, which came upon each other's heels, as the messengers of calamity to Job. We only catch some few sobs from that stricken heart; like the cries of the Crucified from amid the dense gloom of the cross. On first seeing the bloodstained coat, "I will go down into the grave mourning"; on learning the first tidings about the rough governor, the lord of the land, "Me have ye bereaved of my children"; on the appeal of his sons to spare Benjamin, "My son shall not go down with you, lest ye bring down my grey hairs with sorrow to the grave"; on their renewed appeal. "Wherefore dealt ye so ill with me as to tell the man ye had a brother?" On giving his final consent, in addition to the direction that they should take some few delicacies from their almost emptied stores, he said sadly and almost despairingly, "God Almighty give you mercy before the man, that he may send away your other brother, and Benjamin. If I be bereaved of my children, I am bereaved."

But the night of weeping was followed by the morning of joy. Joy looked in at the old man's window; and sorrow and sighing fled away. What a confusion of emotion must have filled his heart when the completed band of his sons stood once again before him with such amazing tidings! Benjamin was there, and Simeon. Love had welded them together in the furnace of sorrow, like a twelve-linked chain, no link of which would ever again be missing. The God of their fathers had met with them; and henceforward would supply their needs so fully, that they could have no further lack, though the famine should last thrice seven years. And, above all, Joseph was yet alive; and he was governor over all the land of Egypt. What wonder that the aged heart stood still, and its machinery almost threatened to break down, beneath the pressure of sudden rapture. At first he could not believe it all. But the sight of the wagons convinced him. Then there came forth a gleam of the royal spirit of faith—the spirit of Jacob revived, and *Israel* said, "It is enough: Joseph my son is yet alive; I will go and see him before I die."

Before he left Canaan, he had one final interview with his Almighty Friend. It happened at Beersheba—the last halting place amid the green pasture lands of the Land of Promise, and before they struck into the sand waste that lay between them and Egypt. Everything there reminded him of his own early life which was spent there. He could find the ruins of his father's altar; and the well which his father had sunk; and "he offered sacrifices unto the God of his father Isaac." At that time his mind was engaged in eager debate as to the path of duty. On the one hand, love to Joseph and his necessities drew him to Egypt; on the other, the memory of how much evil had befallen his ancestors whenever they went down to Egypt, made him eagerly question whether he was justified in going. It was at that time that God made his path clear, by saying, "Fear not to go down into Egypt; for I will there make of thee a great nation: I will go down with thee into Egypt; and Joseph shall put his hand upon thine eyes." How comfortably our God speaks to us when we are sore perplexed. If we will only wait, we shall hear a voice behind us saying, "This is the way, walk ye in it." But, since the voice speaks from behind, we must not run on too far or fast in front.

(1) There is a glimpse of the Israel-nature in his meeting with Joseph. How feverishly the old man anticipated it! And when, on the

confines of Egypt, he learned that the second chariot in the land was bringing his long lost son to his embrace, he roused himself to meet him; not as the Jacob of olden days, but as Israel the Prince. "And Israel said unto Joseph, Now let me die, since I have seen thy face, because thou art yet alive."

(2) There is yet another glimpse of the Israel-nature in his blessing of Pharaoh. Joseph might almost have been ashamed of his aged father, and left him in the background. He was old, and decrepit, and lame. He had spent all his life in tents and sheep farms, and was totally ignorant of the manners of a court. He was an exile, an emigrant, a man who had failed. His very presence there was due to his ruinous losses. What a contrast between him and the glorious Pharaoh, whose court teemed with science and wit; with soldiers and priests; with wealth and splendor! And yet, when he stood before Pharaoh, there was so much moral grandeur about him that the greatest monarch in the world bent eagerly beneath his blessing. "How old art thou?" was the kind inquiry of the mighty monarch, to commemorate whom a massive pyramid, destined to outlast his race, was in course of erection. The question was perhaps suggested by his bent form and withered look. The reply was sad enough; and it was the Jacob-nature that uttered it. It seemed like an anticipation of the cry of Ecclesiastes, "Vanity of vanities, all is vanity." It was lit up by no single ray of thankfulness, or faith, or hope: "My life has been a pilgrimage; its days have been few and evil." *Few,* in comparison with those of Terah, Abraham, and Isaac. *Evil,* in comparison with that of Esau, who stood at the head of a great kingdom, the progenitor of a line of kings. And yet, with this confession ringing in his ears, Pharaoh was blessed by those outstretched trembling hands, and by that quavering voice. Esau never could have done that.

"Without all contradiction the less is blessed of the better." Jacob must have had something about him that rendered him superior to the greatest monarch of his time. There were two kings in that royal chamber decorated by weird hieroglyphs and long lines of fantastic figures: the one, royal with the adventitious distinction of birth and rank; the other, a wayworn pilgrim, royal with the divine patent of royalty—a noble character. And, as they stood together, it was shown to all the

world that the spiritual is greater than the material; and that God can
endow a human spirit with such moral splendor as to compel the
world's conquerors to confess themselves conquered before its power.
You may be crafty, mean, and bargain-loving; yet if you will but yield
yourself to God, and submit to his loving discipline, He will make you
truly royal, and give you the moral power, which masters all other
power beside.

(3) There is yet another glimpse of the Israel-nature in his solemn
injunctions to Joseph about his burial. "The time drew nigh that *Israel*
must die; and he called his son Joseph, and said unto him. . . . And
Israel bowed himself upon the bed's head" (47:29, 30). It is the death
scene which shows the true nature of a man; and its darkness set Jacob's
better nature in full relief.

He was evidently a man of faith. He knew the ancient promise
made by God, of which Abraham may have often spoken to him in his
early life—that their seed should inherit Canaan. He was sure, therefore, that his people would not always abide in Egypt—however fertile
its Goshens, or friendly its peoples. The trumpet would sound the
summons for their departure. If then he were buried in Egypt, he
would be left behind, a stranger among strangers; and this could not be.
He must be where his people were. To him, therefore, burial in the
most splendid mausoleum that was ever constructed to that land of
silent tombs was not for one moment to be compared with burial in
Machpelah's solitary and humble cave; which at that time was a mere
outpost in a distant and hostile land. And he desired it, not only because the mortal remains of Abraham and Sarah, of Isaac and Rebekah,
and of Leah lay there, but because he foresaw the time when it would
be surrounded by the teeming myriads of his children.

He could only see this by faith. He "had not received the promises,
but, by faith, he had seen them afar off, and was persuaded of them,
and embraced them." It was by faith that he was able to say, "Behold I
die: but God shall be with you, and bring you again unto the land of
your father. Bury me not in Egypt, but I will lie with my fathers, and
thou shalt carry me out of Egypt, and bury me in their burying place."
Was it not *Israel* that spoke thus? Faith made him royal; as it will en-
noble the coarsest and commonest nature, lifting the beggar from the

dunghill, and making him sit among princes. And these noble utterances prove how truly God had done his work of ennoblement; and how royal was the spirit of the dying patriarch.

(4) There is yet another glimpse of the Israel-nature in his dealings with Joseph's sons. In the chapter that records that solemn scene, it is almost entirely on Israel that our attention is fixed. "Israel strengthened himself on his bed." "Israel beheld Joseph's sons." "Israel stretched out his right hand." "Israel said unto Joseph."

The sands of time had nearly run out in that aged and battered body; and when Joseph arrived at his dwelling, the gift of his own munificence, the dying man seems to have been lying in the extreme of physical exhaustion. But the sound of the beloved name of "Joseph" rallied him; and, propped by pillows, he sat up upon his bed.

Then, with that wonderful accuracy of memory which is so remarkable in the dying, he reviewed the past. The vision of the wondrous ladder, with its troops of angels; the precious words of promise, which one hundred years could not obliterate from the tablets of memory; the scene on the hilly road to Bethlehem, where he buried Rachel; the successive instance of the guardian care of the Angel who had tended him, as a shepherd does his flock, all his life long until that day—all passed before his eye, dim with age, but bright with memory and hope.

Amid this reverie, the old man became aware of the presence of Joseph's two sons, and inquired who they were; and when he knew, he asked that they might be brought near enough for him to give them an old man's blessing. He did this with great affection and solemnity. He kissed and embraced them; and asked that his good angel might bless the lads. He ranked them among his own sons: and was led by prophetic insight to distinguish between them, crossing his hands, and laying his right on the head of the younger, whom Joseph had placed before his left; and his left on the head of the elder, whom the father had placed before his right. When Joseph remonstrated with him, thinking it was a mistake due to his age and blindness, the old man still held to his choice, as one conscious of a prerogative in which not even Joseph must interfere.

This touching interview ended by the gift to Joseph of the parcel of ground which he had wrested from the Amorites in Shechem. It had long ago returned to its original owners, but he saw, down the vista of the future, that there would be a reversion of the whole to him and his—and it was of that future that he spoke in faith.

The whole of this scene is replete with a dignity, born of moral greatness, and worthy of Israel, the Prince.

Time fails to bring out the traits of royalty in the closing scene of all, which must yield us material for our next chapter. It is enough to remind you of them, ere we close. They are evident enough. Twelve strong, bearded men stand around him. He is in the last extreme of physical decrepitude, but he does not cower or shrink before them, as in other days. His face may be shadowed with death, but his eye gleams with the light of prophecy. He calls out their names one by one. He arraigns them at the bar of judgment. He reviews their past. He apportions them their praise or blame. He allots their future. "These are the twelve tribes of Israel; and this is it that their father spake unto them."

We need not go into further particulars, because enough has been said to convince the most careless reader of the royalty that shone forth from this aged man, as the gleaming torch lights flashed from the breaking pitchers of Gideon's host. And there is enkindled in our hearts the hope that God will do as much for us, through Him who loveth us, and by His death hath made us kings unto God, with whom we shall one day reign on the earth.

Rest,
and the Rest Giver

Oh, the little birds sang east, The little birds sang west!
And I said in underbreath, All our life is mixed with death:
And who knoweth which is best?
Oh, the little birds sang east, The little birds sang west!
And I smiled to think God's good flows Around our incompleteness;
Round our restlessness He's rest!

Mrs. E. B. Browning

Genesis 44

There is much of interest in these dying words of Jacob, through which Israel the Prince shines so conspicuously. We can but touch them as we pass, as the sea bird touches the wave; for higher themes allure us.

It would, for instance, be interesting to mark their accuracy. Reuben, though the firstborn, never excelled; no judge, prophet, or ruler, sprang from his tribe. Simeon was almost absorbed in the nomad tribes, of Southern Palestine. The cities in which the sons of Levi dwelt were scattered throughout all the tribes. Vestiges of terraced vineyards still attest how well the hilly province assigned to Judah suited the culture of the vine. Zebulun embosomed the lake of Galilee, and stretched away toward the coast of the blue Mediterranean. Esdraelon, the battlefield of Palestine, where Assyria from the north and Egypt from the South often met in deadly feud, lay within the limits of Issachar. Dan was small as an adder, but like it, could inflict dangerous wounds on any invader who had to pass by it towards the heart of the country. Gad, much pressed by border war; Asher, notable for fertility; Naphtali, famous for eloquence; Benjamin, cruel as a wolf. All these justified the prophecy of their dying ancestor; while the mighty tribes of Ephraim and Manasseh, sprung from the sons of Joseph, inherited to the full "the blessings of heaven above; blessings of the deep that lieth under; blessings of the breasts and of the womb; blessings to the utmost bound of the everlasting hills."

It would be interesting, also, to mark the beauty of these dying words. They abound in observation and description of animal nature; indicating the habits of the shepherd's life, with which, from his earliest days Jacob must have been familiar. The lion's whelp, couching in his lair, refusing to be roused up, because satisfied with a sufficient meal. The ass, and her colt browsing on the young grapes of the vine. The serpent lurking in the sand; and springing out as the horse passes him, with venomous sting. The wolf, with stealthy tread, seeking his prey at night. The slender, gentle hind. Then, too, the vineyards, rich with grapes, that stain the garments of the peasants with blood-red juice, as they stamp them in the vats. The boughs running over the vineyard walls, in rich bounty, and giving refreshment to weary passers by. The bubbling waters of the spring. The beach of the distant sea. The blue outline of the everlasting hills in the far distance. All these bespeak a mind that loved natural beauty.

It would be interesting, also, to mark the close connection between the awards and the character of the bearded sons who stood around the withered, propped-up body of that dying man; while his spirit was flaming out in one last splendid outburst of prophetic and princelike glory, too much for the frail tenement to endure. Take, for example, the case of Reuben: he had committed a nameless sin years before; he might have hoped that it was all long since forgotten, but no, here it reappears, dragged into inevitable light—as ours must be, unless hidden beneath the Blood of Jesus. That sin deprived him of the primacy—*that one sin*. Was not this arbitrary? Not so: since it was the index of his character, and was the unerring evidence of an unstable nature; for sensuality and instability are one. As sensual indulgence palsies the nerves of the body, so it paralyzes the strength and decision of the spirit. And there was this further dread effect of Reuben's sin: he not only entailed a loss of position and prestige on his descendants, but he transmitted to them his own character. On the threshold of Canaan they asked for land east of Jordan; they could not wait: they showed all the characteristics of the man of appetite, who places the present above the future, and seen above the unseen. And Deborah, in her war song, changed the requiem of the martial valor of the tribe.

But amid all this change of character, condition, and estate, there comes, in these dying words, the announcement of a personality, mysterious, ineffable, sublime, which dwarfs all others—as Mont Blanc the lesser elevations of his mountain realm; and before which that aged spirit bows in worship, illumining the withered face with a light not born of earth. What does he mean by those mystic words, describing the Shiloh; and His coming; and the gathering of the peoples to Him? There is a power in them that strangely stirs our spirits. We feel instinctively that we are face to face with Him before whom angels bow, veiling their faces with their wings. Again the words ring in our hearts: "The scepter shall not depart from Judah, nor a lawgiver from between his feet, until Shiloh come; and unto Him shall the gathering of the peoples be."

I. LET US TRY TO UNDERSTAND THEM. The primacy of Israel, forfeited by Reuben, was transferred to Judah. The scepter, or staff, surely indicates legislative authority; the lawgiver, some kind of legislator: and the drift of meaning in the verse is that Judah should retain the primacy of the tribes; and should not fail to have some kind of government, and some kind of governor, until One came, of whom Jacob spoke as Shiloh.

And who is this Shiloh? The greatest modern Hebrew critics tell us that it is like the German *Frederick*—Rich in Peace; the Rest Giver; the Man of Rest. And of whom can this be true, but of One? Amid the vice and crimes of their times, an aged pair gave to their newborn son the name of Noah—*Rest*; and hoped that he would live to comfort them. It was, alas! a vain hope; the waters of the deluge were destined to sweep over their home and world. No *man* can give us rest. He who shall give rest to the toiling populations of earth, must be more than man; and must be superior to those changes that toss us on their tumultuous billows. The true Shiloh can be none other than the Son of God; who, standing among earth's toiling millions, said, "Come unto Me, all ye that labor and are heavy laden, and I will give you rest."

I have sometimes wondered where Jacob learned this most sweet and true name of our Lord Jesus. Was it flashed into his heart, at that moment, for the first time? It may have been. But there is another supposition which has often pleased me. You will remember that at Peniel, Jacob asked the mysterious combatant His name. What answer did he receive? When Manoah asked a similar question, the angel of the Lord told him it was secret. But no such negative was spoken to Jacob. The angel simply said: "Wherefore is it that thou dost ask after My name? And he blessed him there." I have sometimes thought that, as He blessed him, He whispered in his ear this lovely title; which lingered in the old man's mind, as the years went on, and became invested with ever fuller and richer meaning, as he felt to need more urgently the balm and strength which it contained. To him that overcomes Christ promises to give a white stone; and in that stone a new name written, which is only known to him that receives it. Why should He not have done as much for that old world patriarch, who had overcome in his defeat; and had gone from wrestling in full strength to halting on shrunken thigh? And it would be only natural that, at the moment of full surrender, He should teach him the secret of rest. This is the universal order of Christian living: first the resistance; then the shrunken sinew; then the yielding and clinging; and finally rest.

Jacob, then, believed that the Rest Giver would come at length; and that, when He came, people would be gathered to Him—not driven, as he had seen long strings of Nubian slaves driven through the streets of Egyptian towns: but gathered as a hen gathers her chickens beneath her wing; or as the magnet attracts steel filings to itself.

II. LET US NOTE, ALSO, THEIR LITERAL FULFILLMENT. For long centuries, Judah held the proud position assigned by the dying chieftain. The lion of the tribe of Judah brooked no rival. Jerusalem lay in his territory. David sprang from his sons. Throughout the long captivity, princes still claimed and held their right; for we are told, when Cyrus issued the proclamation that gave them liberty, "there arose up the chief of the fathers of Judah, and numbered unto them Sheshbazzar, the prince of Judah." It was Judah that returned from the captivity and gave the title *Jew* to every member of the race; and even up to the times of our Lord, there were vestiges of the ancient government in the council before which He was arraigned.

But the system had become decrepit, and showed signs of passing away. We are told, for instance, when the Idumean Herod was placed upon the throne, all Jewish patriots were in deep consternation. Men with wild and haggard looks, their garments rent, and ashes on their heads, went about the streets crying, "Woe unto us! Woe unto us! For the scepter is departed from Judah; and a lawgiver from between his feet." Still the complex machinery of inferior and superior courts lingered on, until that mighty explosion burst beneath the Jewish State—leaving not a single Jew within fifty miles of Bethlehem; and making it utterly impossible for Shiloh to come out of Judah.

Before this entire breakup of the Jewish system, the Shiloh came. When they were expecting Him at the front door, He stole in the back. While they were expecting Him with outward show, He came as the spring comes, and as day breaks. He had rest in Himself. What else could have kept Him so calm—amid the tumult at Nazareth; and the raging of the storm on the Lake of Galilee; and the mob in Gethsemane? And He gave rest: rest from weary years of pain; rest from tears and heartache; rest from sin.

And as He has spoken through the centuries, His still small voice has been heard above the fevered throb and pulse of human life, saying, "Come unto Me, come unto Me!" and spirits have arisen and gone forth to Him: drawn to Him as the publicans and sinners were of old; gathering to Him as the oppressed in the old kingdom of Saul gathered to David in Adullam's cave, furnishing material for a host which was to carry everything before its victorious arms. "Thy people shall be free will offerings in the day of thy power."

III. LET US REALIZE THEIR TRUTH. What a variety of weary eyes will read these words—weary eyes, aching heads, tired bodies, breaking hearts! Tired of sitting at the task which barely suffices to get bread for hungry little ones; tired of waiting for one who never comes; tired of hearing the slow torture of never-ceasing pain: tired of the strain of competition, ever waxing keener and more merciless; tired of the conflict against the evil around; tired of the war with self and sin within; tired of life—

> Lord, oftentimes I am a weary quite
> Of my own self, my sin, my vanity;
> Yet be not Thou (or I am lost outright)
> Weary of me.

Would to God that each of these could understand that Jesus Christ, the true Shiloh, is able to give them, now and forevermore—rest! "Come unto Me, *all* ye that are heavy laden, and I will give you REST."

It is a royal word. If this were the only scrap of His words, we should feel Him to have been the most royal man that ever trod our world. He knows exactly what men want; and He feels that He has the secret, and is Himself the universal and unfailing reservoir of rest. What must not be the ocean fullness of His heart—which can fill up every void and vacancy in all human spirits: as the tides of the Pacific, the stormless, restful ocean, fill up all the myriad indentations of every continent, and coral reef, and emerald isle, washed by their waves! What certainty is here! No doubt, or question, or fear of failure; no faltering in that clear voice; no hesitancy in that decisive accent. We may trust Him, brothers and sisters. He at least has learned the law of equilibrium. He speaks that which He knows. He has Himself the rest He promises. Put yourselves into His hand. It will not take Him longer to give you rest, than it took Him to still the waves; they did not even need to rock themselves to rest: "*Immediately* there was a great calm."

The Shiloh-rest is not for heaven. We need not ask for the wings of a dove to fly away to it. We should not find it hereafter, if we did not first find it here. "We which believe DO enter into rest." The rest remains, only in the sense of being unexhausted by all who have gone before. It awaits us in unstinted abundance.

The Shiloh-rest is not in Circumstances. That thought lies at the root of the teaching of the Epicurean, the Stoic, the worldly philosopher. But circumstances will never bring it; any more than change of posture will bring permanent relief to the pain-racked body. Here is a truer science: rest within—rest within the heart, while storms, and perplexities, and trials are swirling through the world; as the ocean depths are still enough to permit of perpetual deposits while hurricanes sweep the surface; and as there is a point of calm in the midst of the fiercest whirlwind that ever marched across the desert sands.

The Shiloh-rest is not in Inaction. He invites us to no bank of roses; to no Elysian plain; to no parade ground. In heaven, though they rest, yet they rest not. They rest in their blessed service. They serve without breaking their rest. There is the strenuous putting forth of energy, but no strain, no effort, no sense of fatigue. And such is the rest He gives. Does He not speak of a "burden" and a "yoke" in the same breath as He speaks of Rest?

And it is not hard to get it. See! He *gives* it; and it does not need much effort to take a gift. He shows just where to look for it; and it is easy enough to *find* a thing if we know just where it lies. There seems to be but three conditions to be fulfilled by us.

(1) *Surrender all to Him.* As long as you try to wield that scepter, or permit your will to be the lawgiver of your life, the Shiloh cannot come to you. You must give up your own efforts to save yourself—your own ideas of getting right with God; your own choice; your own way; your own will. You must as absolutely cease from your own works as God did from His on the Sabbath of His rest. You must hand over your sinful spirit to be saved by Him; you must surrender the keys of every room in your heart; you must be willing for Him to be supreme monarch of every province of your being; you must lie naked and open to Him as the victim before the priest. So only can you expect rest. And if you cannot bring your nature into this posture, ask Him to do it for you. Let your will crown Him—as our own Alfred was crowned, when most of England was still ravaged by the Danes. He will not fail nor be discouraged, till He hath put down all rule and authority and power, and made Himself supreme throughout heart and life.

(2) *Trust Him, by handing over all to Him.* Hand over to Him all your sins and all your sorrows. He takes away the sin of the world. Do not wait till sins have accumulated into a cloud or a mountain. Do not

tarry till the time has come for evening prayer. Do not delay till you are alone. But as swiftly as you are conscious of any burden, pass it on to Jesus; cast all your care upon Him, for he cares for you. His eye is quick to see each effort to believe; and His heart is large enough to hold the troubles of the world. So soon as you give, He takes; and what He takes He also undertakes; and will see it made right for you, to your rejoicing and to His glory. This is the Blessed Rest of Faith; the Land of Promise into which our Joshua waits to lead all who trust Him.

(3) *Take His yoke, and learn of Him*—i.e., do as He did. What did He do? What was His yoke? A yoke means submission. To whom did He submit? Not to man; not even to His mother, not the suggestions of Satan: but to the Father's will. Whenever He saw the handwriting of that will, He meekly yielded submission. This was the secret of His rest. To live in the will of God—this is rest. Be ever on the outlook for it: in every event; in every kindness or insult; in every letter; in every new friendship; in every discipline of Providence; and in every test of Scripture. And whenever you see it, *take it.* Do not wait for it to be forced on you; as a yoke on a heifer unaccustomed to it, which struggles till a deep wound is cut in its flesh. But *take* the yoke; be meek and lowly; imitate Him who said, "The cup which my Father hath given me, shall I not drink it?" The language which best befits such a one is that wonderful sentence, in which simplicity and sublimity struggle for mastery: "Even so, Father; for so it seemed good in Thy sight."

A gentleman once visited a school of deaf and dumb children, and was asked to write them a question on the blackboard; and he wrote: "Why did God make you deaf and dumb, while I can hear and speak?" Tears filled their eyes; and after a slight pause, a little boy stepped forward, and took the chalk and wrote beneath, "Even so, Father; for so it seemed good in Thy sight." If you can say that, you have learned the secret of rest; and Shiloh has already come to you; and you are one of those that are being gathered to Him through the long weary ages to share His ultimate triumph and reign.

❦ 15
Home: At Last!

What is death? Oh, what is death?
'Tis slumber to the weary;
'Tis rest to the forlorn;
'Tis shelter to the dreary;
'Tis peace amid the storm;
'Tis the entrance to our home;
'Tis the passage to that God
Who bids His children come,
When their weary course is trod.
Anonymous

Genesis 50

The end is come at last! And we stand with those stalwart men in that heiroglyph-covered chamber, silent with the hush of death, to see the wayworn pilgrim breathe his last. His life has been a stern fight; his pathway not strewn with roses, but set with flints; few and evil the days of the years of his pilgrimage. Compared with the brilliant career of Esau, his life might be almost considered a failure—estimating it by all human standards of failure and success. But as the scaffold is taken down piece by piece, we catch glimpses of the real manhood which God has been so carefully building up, through long years of pain and sorrow; and as it comes into view, we feel that it is more than enough to justify all. Better a hundredfold to be Israel the Prince, though an exile; than Esau, the founder of a line of dukes. The glory of moral and spiritual rank will glisten when the crowns of earthly splendor shall have moldered into dust; and the name of Israel will be an unfailing inspiration to those who, conscious of untold weakness and unloveableness, shall yet strive to apprehend that for which they were originally apprehended by Christ Jesus.

We, too, if the Lord tarry, shall lie someday in a chamber of death, surrounded by our dear ones. Our spirits must poise themselves for their final flight, and stand waiting at the Beautiful Gate of the temple of life. And as Jacob has taught us how to live, so let him teach us how to die. "Come," said the dying Havelock to his son, "and see how a Christian can die." Some such summons calls us now: for even we, living in the noontide of the Gospel, may obtain salutary hints for our own death hour from one who once seemed to mean to teach us anything, but who now, through the stern discipline of the Angel of Love, stands forth to lead faithful souls through the dark gorge of death into the land of the eternal morning.

Before the mind of the dying patriarch three visions seemed to float in that solemn hour. He was thinking of the City of God; and of the gathering of his clan; and of that lone and distant cave in Canaan where his fathers lay, and which he had so often visited.

I. THE CITY OF GOD. We are expressly told in the Epistle to the Hebrews that Jacob was one of those "who died in faith." He was the heir of Promise. The land promised to Abraham and Isaac had not as yet passed into his possession; it was still held by the wandering and settled tribes, who had eyed his journeyings with such evident suspicion. All he had was the assured promise that in the coming days it should be his through his seed. Perhaps, in the dawn of early vigor, he may have hoped to live until those fair pasture lands and terraced hills had literally passed into his possession. The yearning comes out in the deep drawn ejaculation, flashing through his dying charge to his sons, "I have waited for Thy salvation, O Lord!"

But as the years passed on, and clouds closed over this azure aperture of earthly hope, he was compelled to realize that he would never live to be lord of Canaan. Nevertheless, he clung tenaciously to the blessed promise, so often reiterated to Abraham, that the land should become his people's; and his assurance that God would keep His word flung a radiance, which neither sorrow nor adversity could dim, over his dying moments. Oh, glorious faith! It carries a torch through the long catacombs of sorrow, keeping the heart from fainting, until the welcome dawn of accomplishment grows upon the sight. What cannot faith do for those whom God has taught to trust! "My soul, wait thou only upon God; for my expectation is from Him."

As it became clear to Jacob that *he* was not to inherit Canaan, he seems to have fixed his mind with increasing eagerness on heaven. He felt that if God had not destined for him an earthly resting place, yet He had prepared for him a City. Its foundations had not been laid by man; its walls bore no mark of human workmanship; its atmosphere could not be stained with the smoke or dust of earth. And it was for that glorious city, the city of the saints, that his pilgrim spirit now yearned. It was the vision of that city which had enabled him to confess to the mighty Pharaoh that he was a pilgrim and a stranger on the earth. And now it was his close proximity to it that stirred his aged spirit, and drew it on with breathless eagerness and rapid steps.

The sacred writer employs a beautiful similitude when he says of Jacob and the rest of the patriarchs, that they greeted the promises from afar (Heb. 11:13). When the traveler returns from distant lands, and from the summit of some neighboring hill catches the first glimpse of his still distant home, with its spiral column of blue smoke curling up amid the trees, he is disposed to fall upon the greensward, and with outstretched hands thank God and greet his home. "Hail! Happy scenes of childhood; and blest abode of manhood's prime." So Jacob, as he neared the City of God, so dear to faithful hearts, approved his kinsmanship with the elect spirits of all ages, by reaching forth towards it his aged, trembling hands. And as God looked down upon that eager attitude of faith, and hope, and desire, He was not ashamed to be called his God.

Modern commentators have wrangled fiercely as to how much or how little of the future life was realized by these ancient saints. Into that controversy I have no desire to enter. But I find a large answer to their questions in the assurance of Scripture, that Jacob and the men of his type desired "the better country, that is, a heavenly." The future was less indistinct to them than we sometimes suppose. They, too, stood on Pisgah heights and beheld a Land of Promise: not that on which the veteran lawgiver gazed, bounded by the blue waters of the Mediterranean, but that which is never shadowed by night, or swept by wild tempests of wind and rain—the true Home of the saints. On such a Pisgah height Jacob was standing; and as all earthly objects, even the face of Joseph, grew indistinct to his dimming eyes, those rapturous and celestial scenes grew upon his spiritual vision, and beckoned to him.

In what relation do you, my readers, stand to that City of God? Do not imagine that it will gladden your dying gaze, unless it has often been the object of your loving thought in the days of health and vigor. Your citizenship must be in heaven now, if you would feel attracted to it as your true home at last. Is it so? Do you feel content to live in tents, having no fixed hold upon this fleeting scene; and confessing yourselves pilgrims and strangers on the earth—because you are looking for the City? Do you feel the *pull* of that city, as the sailor does of the anchor, which keeps him from drifting with the tide? Do you anticipate it, like the children in the Children's Crusade, who asked of every city they entered, "Is this Jerusalem?" If so, it shall gladden your dying moments. You shall see the holy city descending out of heaven from God, as a bank seems to approach the nearing vessel. And you shall have the blessedness, assured by the living Savior to those who wash their robes, of the right to enter in, through the gates, into the City (Rev. 22:14, R.V.).

II. THE GATHERING OF THE CLAN. "I am to be gathered unto my people." When the dying patriarch spoke thus, he meant something more than that his dust should mingle with all that was mortal of his forefathers. He expresses that thought in the following sentence: "Bury me with my fathers." No; he meant something more than this. He surely looked upon the City as the gathering place of his clan; the metropolis of true and godly hearts; the *rendezvous* of all who were *his* people, because they were people of God.

How much truer is this thought of heaven than that which is entertained by many Christian people! "What do you think of the intermediate state?" "Shall we be consciously happy from the very moment of death?" "Shall we know one another on the other side?" These are the doleful questions asked on many sides; and they present a melancholy contrast to the words of the dying Jacob, "I am to be gathered unto my people."

What as to the intermediate state? At the best "we know not what we shall be." We cannot penetrate the veil that only opens wide enough to admit the entering spirit. It is clear that our spirits will not reach their full consummation and bliss till the morning of the resurrection, when body and spirit will be reunited, but it is equally clear that they will not be unconscious, but will enter into the blessed presence of our Lord.

This was taught by Christ Himself, when He quoted the words, "I am the God of Abraham, Isaac, and Jacob"; and added the comment, "He is not the God of the dead, but of the living." That grand formula was spoken years after Jacob had fallen asleep; and yet God speaks of Himself as his God: and since He could not be the God of dead mummies only, or of unconscious spirits, Jacob and all the rest must have been living. Yes, they were living then, and are living now, possessed of all the vivid life that made them what they were.

There is no accent of uncertainty in the New Testament. As soon as the tent is taken down, the mansion is entered (2 Cor. 5:2). Absent from the body, the believer is present with the Lord. "To die is gain"; which were an impossibility if the spirit did not have more of Christ than is possible on this side of the Golden City (Phil. 1:21). The dying Stephen went direct into the hands of his Lord (Acts 7:59). Do not puzzle over useless questionings: be content to know that death is not a state, but an act; not a resting place, but a transition; a passage, a birth, a crossing the Bridge of Sighs from the prison to the palace.

> Death is another life. We bow our heads
> At going out, we think; and enter straight
> Another golden chamber of the King's,
> Larger than this we leave, and lovelier.

What as to the recognition of the departed? It would not have been an object of anticipation to Jacob to be gathered to his people, if he would not know them when he reached their blessed society. When the Jew thought of the unseen world, he expected to meet the saints, of whom he had been wont to hear from childhood, and especially Abraham. Was not the Jew wiser than most Christians? What! has the body powers of recognition, and the spirit none? Shall love, which has molded the life, range through eternity unable to find the twin spirit with which it had become entwined? Can that be a Father's home, where the brothers and sisters do not know each other?

But these questions have always been solved, to me at least, by a careful study of the facts of our Lord's resurrection body—the model to the likeness of which we are to be conformed (Phil. 3:21). Those who knew Him before His death, recognized Him after. His very voice had in it intonations familiar to those who loved Him (John 20:16). His mannerisms were identical; and sufficient to identify Him to the two disciples with whom He sat (Luke 24:31). And as it was with Him, so shall it be with us and our beloved.

We shall be gathered to our people. Death will not usher us into a chill, unfriendly circle, but into a great gathering of loving and sympathizing friends, who shall give us a choral welcome as we enter into the eternal kingdom of our Lord (2 Pet. 1:11; see the Greek).

Throughout the ages the elect souls of our race have been gathering there. Are they our people? Can we claim kinship with them. There is but one bond, as we are taught in Hebrews 11. That bond is not of dispensation; or of knowledge; or of exploits, but of faith—such faith as may exist in a beggar or a king, in a child or a philosopher. It is independent of age, or sect, or knowledge, or work. But, wherever it is found, it designates the owner to be one of those who can claim kinship with the saintly inhabitants of the City of God. The test question of qualification for the franchise of the New Jerusalem is: "Dost thou believe in the name of the only begotten Son of God?"

III. THE CAVE OF MACHPELAH. "Bury me with my fathers in the cave that is in the field of Ephron the Hittite." For seventeen years he had lived in Egypt, surrounded by all the comforts that Joseph's filial love could devise, and his munificence execute. He must have become familiar with Egypt's splendid temples and obelisks and pyramids, with which that cave could not for one moment be compared. But he would not rest in any of them. He must be laid where Abraham and Sarah, Isaac and Rebekah, and the faithful Leah awaited resurrection.

This was something more than the natural sentiment which impels us to request burial in some quiet spot in God's acre, where our family name is inscribed on many of the gravestones around. He felt that Machpelah's cave was the first outpost in the land which was one day to belong to his people; and he wanted, so far as he might, to be there with them, and to share in the land of promise.

The last word was spoken, the last commission given, and he knew the end was come. "He gathered up his feet into the bed"; *i.e.*, he met death quietly, calmly, manfully. He was not dragged away as a criminal; he went to meet it with complacency and with joy. The servant might have a grim face and a sable suit, but he had come to take him home. He quietly breathed out his spirit, and was gathered unto his people. And at that moment sorrow and sighing which had been his close companions in life, fled away forever.

How calm and noble that face looked, fixed in the marble of death! The Jacob-look had vanished from it; and it was stamped with the smile with which the royal Israel-spirit had molded it in its outward passage.

> So, pilgrim, now thy brows are cold,
>> We see thee what thou art; and know
>> Thy likeness to the wise below,
> Thy kindred to the great of old.

What wonder, then, that Joseph fell upon his father's face, and wept upon him, and kissed him! He had borne the strain as long as he could; and now nature must vent herself in manly, filial grief.

The body was carefully embalmed. No time, or pains, or cost, were spared. Egypt herself mourned for him for seventy days. And then one of the most splendid funeral processions that ever gathered to lay saint, or sage, or hero to his rest, carried that precious casket in solemn pomp from Egypt up to Canaan. The chivalry of Egypt, its statesmen and counselors, its princes and priests, joined with the shepherds of Goshen in accompanying the *cortége*. And the signs of mourning were so great as to impress the inhabitants of the land, the Canaanites.

The stone was rolled away, and the remains laid on their appointed niche; and in all probability they are there, in a state of perfect preservation, unto this day. Many a storm has swept over them—Assyrian, Egyptian, Babylonian, Grecian, Roman, Saracenic, and Mohammedan. But nought has disturbed their quiet rest; and they hold the land in fee, till God shall fulfill, in all its magnificence, the promise which He made and has never recalled—that He would give the land to Jacob's seed for an everlasting inheritance. So rest thee, ISRAEL, THE PRINCE!

The God of Jacob

With all thy heart, with all thy soul and mind,
Thou must Him love, and His behests embrace;
All other loves—with which the world doth blind
Weak fancies, and stir up affections base—
Thou must renounce, and utterly displace;
And give thyself unto Him full and free,
That full and freely Gave Himself to thee.
Spenser

Psalm 46

I t is very comforting to discover in how many parts of Scripture God calls Himself the God of Jacob. He seems to take special delight in the title which links His holy nature with one who, so far from giving promise of saintship, was naturally one of the meanest of men. We should not have been surprised to find Him speaking of Himself as the God of Israel, the Prince, but it is as startling as it is reassuring to find Him speaking of Himself still more often as the God of Jacob.

But as we notice the careful reiteration of the designation—especially in the Psalms of David and the prophecies of Isaiah—we learn this priceless lesson: that He has not changed since He took Jacob in hand; that He feels towards such characters now as He did when He began his gracious work of renewal in that poor cramped heart; and that He is ready to do as much for all who are conscious of being equally worthless by nature, and who are willing to put themselves into His gracious hands—which reach down from heaven to earth, "molding men."

There is little doubt that God would do as much for all the readers of these lines, if only they were willing. And it is the object of this closing appeal to urge my readers to let Him have His gracious way with them. As we have studied together Jacob's life and character, have you not been keenly conscious of similarities between him and yourself? *You* too may be cunning, crafty, and deceitful; or you may be prone to outbursts of ungovernable temper; or you may be cursed by unholy desires that honeycomb your better nature; or you may be constantly brought into captivity to some tyrannous sin. Now there is no need for this to be your hapless lot for one moment longer, if only you will hand yourself over to the mighty God of Jacob.

At the door of a mission hall in a low and degraded neighborhood, a Christian man, one evening, was inviting the passersby to go in to the service, which was about to commence. "But my coat is in rags," replied a wretched looking man. "That is no matter," was the answer; "there's a man inside *without a coat at all.*" It was quite enough to remove all further hesitation; and he entered. Forgive the simple illustration by which I wish to press home my meaning on those who may question if their nature is not too ignoble, and their evil habits too confirmed, for them to entertain the hope of saintliness. Your case is not hopeless. If God could make a prince of Jacob, He can do as much for anyone. It is hardly possible for one of us to be more hopeless than Jacob was to begin with; and the same Lord who was so rich in mercy to him, will be as rich to all them that call upon Him in truth.

I. CULTIVATE A HOLY AMBITION. There is no tendency of the unrenewed heart more subtle or dangerous than ambition. "By this sin fell the angels." And yet, if it is properly curbed and kept, ambition plays a useful part among the motive forces of human life. It is a bad sign when a lad, or a man, has no desire to improve his position and get on. In all likelihood he will always lie with the rest of the rabble at the bottom of the hill, without the desire or power to stir. And it is well to cultivate a holy ambition to be all that God can make us; to grasp all the possibilities that lie within the reach of faith; and to apprehend that for which we have been apprehended of Christ Jesus.

Such an ambition fired the heart of the Apostle when he said: "Not as though I had already attained, either were already perfect, but I follow after: . . . forgetting those things which are behind, and reaching forth unto those things which are before, I press toward the mark for the prize of the high calling of God in Christ Jesus" (Phil. 3:12–14). Does not this stir you? Do not be content to be always a Jacob. Do not settle down to lifelong slavery beneath your merciless oppressors. Do not suppose that you must always be what you have been. "The arrows are beyond thee"; make for them!

This holy ambition may be aroused by the study of Christian biography. Every time you read or hear of God's grace being magnified in some beautiful and noble life, thank Him; let your own ideal be raised, and ask Him to do as much for you. But there is nothing which will quicken this sacred spark into a flame so soon as the devout study of the Bible. There are such wonderful openings up of the possibilities of Christian living and being in almost every paragraph. Constant familiarity may have rubbed them bright and smooth, like some well worn coin, but if only we will let the Holy Ghost recut them for us, we shall be perfectly astonished. And as, one after another, these ideals of God's own heart open to our gaze, let us entreat Him "to fulfill in us the good pleasure of His goodness, and the work of faith with power."

Let this be deeply engraven on your heart, as the sacred page is turned—that every promise is for you; and that God is able to do exceeding abundantly above all you can ask or think; and then look up to Him, and claim that He should do as He has said.

II. MAKE A COMPLETE SURRENDER TO GOD. Before God will commence His gracious work on a human spirit, it must be entirely surrendered to Him. The key of every room, and closet, and cupboard, in the being must be put into His hands. Every province of the life must be placed under His government. There must be no keeping back, no reserve: to withhold one thing, even the least, will vitiate the whole transaction; and leave a foothold for the self life from which it will speedily spread back throughout the whole nature.

Who would take a house recently infected by smallpox unless the whole of it were thrown freely open to the officers of health? Who would pretend to advise a friend involved in financial difficulties, unless the whole of his liabilities were freely disclosed? Who would prescribe for a disease, unless the patient told all the symptoms and entirely gave up all other means of cure? And so God will not undertake the case of any poor child of His unless there be first a complete and entire surrender of the whole being to His gentle healing work.

Some time ago, as I was passing down one of the poorer streets in Leicester, I remarked a notice in the window of a most dilapidated shop, the trade of which had for some time past been ebbing away. The notice was to the following effect: "This shop will shortly be opened under entirely new management." And as I stood for a moment there, it seemed as if the whole building put on a kind of hopeful smile, as much as to say, "I am so glad that I am to be put under an entirely fresh managment." Several days afterwards, as I passed that way again, I found a small army of whitewashers and paperhangers at work; and on the next occasion, the change in management was evident to the most casual eye, for the whole place had a clean, sweet look about it which was quite attractive.

Now this is just what you require—you with the Jacob nature. You have been trying to manage yourself all too long. A change is evidently needed, but it must be complete. There must be nothing left of yourself at all. Everything must be absolutely surrendered to that mighty God of Jacob whom the Psalmist made his refuge; and who is able to take bankrupt souls, and make them heirs of God, and joint heirs with Christ. Why should you not make that surrender now?

Instances crowd upon my pen, eagerly asking mention, of those who have entered into experiences of undreamt of blessing through the strait gate of entire surrender. But I forbear to give them here. It is enough to point the way; and leave all to enter the golden land who will.

When you come to the point of self-surrender, it is highly probable that some one thing will suggest itself to your mind which it is very difficult to transfer from your control to that of the Lord Jesus. You would so much prefer to retain it under your own management. You are not quite sure whether He may not introduce some sweeping, and painful changes. You stand in dread, as the lad before he throws himself into the buoyant waves. But such fears are most unworthy of our loving Master. He will take away nothing which it will do us no harm to keep. He never amputates a limb without using some anodyne to lessen the pain without injuring the health. He will never give us one thrill of anguish from which it would be possible to save us.

Do not be afraid of giving all up to the lovely will of Him who is love; and who will not break the bruised reed or quench the smoking flax. If your child were to say, "I am going to give my life over to your ordering; do all you will," would you begin to make him miserable? Would you not rejoice in the opportunity of arresting him in courses which were harming him? Would you not gladly embrace the opportunity of filling him with joys that he could never have realized for himself? And your heavenly Father will not do less for you; only trust Him with all.

And should there be things in your life which you find it hard to abandon—dear as right eye, or hand, or foot; involving the happiness of others as well as your own—tell God that you give them over to Him; and that you are willing to have His will done, if He only will bring it to pass in His own good time and way. And if you cannot say as much as that, tell Him *that you are willing to be made willing:* hand over your will to Him, though it seem to be as a piece of cold, hard iron; sure that He can soften and weld it into the pattern on which He has set His heart.

> Renew my will from day to day;
> Blend it with Thine, and take away
> All that now makes it hard to say,
> Thy will be done.

There is even a more excellent way than any, which is within the reach of the feeblest hand; and that is to ask the Lord to come into your life *to take* that which you do not feel able to give. The only matter of which you need be careful, is your willingness that He should have all; if that is assured, the rest may be safely left to His gracious arrangement. Directly you are willing, the door is opened to Him, and He instantly takes full possession.

III. Be Careful Not to Thwart God's Good Workmanship. Of course, there is a sense in which we cannot resist or impede the execution of His sovereign will. "He doeth as He will amongst the armies of heaven and the inhabitants of earth." And yet, on the other hand, we may hinder and counterwork His loving purposes, "How often would I . . . but ye would not!" Let us be on the guard against this disastrous resistance; and be ever on the alert to work out that which God is working in us, "both to will and to do."

Once, the prophet Jeremiah was led to go down into the valley where the potter was at work, molding clay on a wheel (Jer. 18). And as he stood by to watch the skillful manipulation of the clay, the prophet had, of course, no idea what pattern was in the designer's mind; though, probably, it was one of the noblest conception, and destined for some royal or special purpose. And so, beneath those rapid revolutions of the wheel, the ideal began to take shape. Then suddenly the clay was taken from the wheel with an exclamation of disappointment, and the design was foiled and spoiled. Why? Because the potter was wanting in skill? No, but because the clay refused to take on the shape which he had designed. His work was, therefore, marred on the wheel; and he was compelled to make of that clay some inferior vessel from that which he had intended. It might have served a noble purpose in the royal household, or even in the Temple service, but it was now fashioned into a coarser form, for some mean purpose in a peasant's home. The lesson was meant for Israel, but it will serve for us.

Speaking after the manner of men, may we not say that when God created us anew in Christ Jesus He conceived a noble ideal, after the pattern of which we might have been conformed? And if we had only yielded to Him more completely, that ideal would long ago have revealed itself in our experience. But alas! We have not always been plastic in His hands; we have not obeyed the promptings of His Spirit; we have quenched and grieved Him; and we are far different today from what we might have been, and from what God intended us to become. Shall we not confess this with tears and shame? Shall we not take unto us words, and turn to Him, saying, "Now, O Lord, we are the clay, and Thou our potter; we are all the work of Thy hands. Be not wroth very sore." And if a man purify himself from the sins which have hindered the Divine Workman, he shall yet become "a vessel unto honor, sanctified, and meet for the Master's use, and prepared unto every good work."

I do not deny that God will fulfill His purpose in us, even though we hinder Him, but it will be carried through, as it was in the case of Jacob, at a terrible expenditure of agony, and the shriveling of the sinew of our strength. The yoke will have to be borne, and the long furrows cut; and if the unaccustomed heifer prove restive, its struggles will only chafe sores about its neck—but it will ultimately be broken in. On the whole, therefore, it is always better to *take* the yoke of Divine purpose, offered by our Lord as His: "Take *My* yoke." And remember, a yoke is for two. Our Lord yokes Himself at our side; and paces by us, step by step, doing for us what Simon the Cyrenian once did for Him, on the way to Golgotha.

IV. SEEK THE FULLNESS OF THE SPIRIT. That Spirit dwelt in Israel; as the sun flushes the topmost summits of the Alps with a roseate glow, long before it bathes the valleys in its meridian light. But in this blessed dispensation, He is given—not to saints and prophets only, but to all: to sons and daughters; to old men and children; to servants and handmaidens. "The promise is to you and to your children; and to all that are afar off, even as many as the Lord our God shall call" (Acts 2:39). And it is only as we receive this sacred gift, in all its fullness, that we can hope to attain to the royal standard of the Israel-life. That blessed Spirit is the Spirit of the Son—the Spirit of the one royal Man that ever walked the world; and if we would have His nature, we must have His Spirit: not in drops, but in rivers; not as a zephyr breath, but as "a rushing mighty wind."

This is the dying need of the Christian Church in this country. We have learning, rhetoric, fashion, wealth, splendid buildings, and superb machinery, but we are powerless, for lack of the power which can only be obtained through the fullness of the Spirit. Of what use is a train of sumptuous Pullman cars without an engine throbbing with the power of steam? We have too largely forgotten the exhortation; "Be filled with the Spirit." We have thought that the fullness of the Spirit was a specialty for the apostolic age, instead of being for all time. And thus the majority of Christians are living on the other side of Pentecost. We can never be what we might be until we have got back to apostolic theory and practice in respect to this all-essential matter. Oh that God, in these last days, would raise up some fire-touched tongue to do for this neglected doctrine what Luther did for justification by faith!

In the meanwhile seek this blessed filling. It is only possible to emptied hearts, but just so soon as a vacuum has been created by the act of entire surrender, there will be an instantaneous filling by the Holy Ghost in answer to expectant desire and eager faith. For the Holy Ghost longs to enter the human heart; resembling in this the air, which is ever seeking to enter our homes by every keyhole, crack, and aperture. Do not wait to *feel* that you have Him. Be sure that you do possess His fullness, if only you have made room for Him; and go on acting in the strength of His mighty power. So shall you be an Israel, and have power with God and man.

The words, of course, apply only to those who by faith have become the justified children of God. If any who are not assured of this should have read thus far, let them now make a complete abandonment of themselves to the Son of God, to be saved by His death and life, just as He will. This is the first essential step towards royalty. To as many as receive Him, to them He gives the right to become children of God, even to as many as believe on His name (John 1:12).

Life is not child's play to those who enter into God's purposes, and in whom He is fulfilling His sublime ideals. But, with the dying Kingsley, we are sure that all is right and well since "all is under law." When the discipline is over, we shall be more than satisfied with the result; and, taking our stand among the princes of the royal blood, we shall ascribe eternal glory to Him who loved us in spite of all, and washed us from our sins in His own blood, and out of Jacobs made us KINGS UNTO GOD.

CPSIA information can be obtained at www.ICGtesting.com
Printed in the USA
LVOW10s2046170316

479640LV00016B/58/P

Made in the USA
Coppell, TX
20 April 2022